MW00780143

DESIGN THINKING

Design thinking is a powerful process that facilitates understanding and framing of problems, enables creative solutions, and may provide fresh perspectives on our physical and social landscapes. Not just for architects or product developers, design thinking can be applied across many disciplines to solve real-world problems and reconcile dilemmas. It is a tool that may trigger inspiration and the imagination, and lead to innovative ideas that are responsive to the needs and issues of stakeholders.

Design Thinking: A Guide to Creative Problem Solving for Everyone will assist in addressing a full spectrum of challenges from the most vexing to the everyday. It renders accessible the creative problem-solving abilities that we all possess by providing a dynamic framework and practical tools for thinking imaginatively and critically. Every aspect of design thinking is explained and analyzed together with insights on navigating through the process.

The application of design thinking to help solve myriad problems that are *not* typically associated with design is illuminated through vignettes drawn from such diverse realms as politics and society, business, health and science, law, and writing. A combination of theory and application makes this volume immediately useful and personally relevant.

Andrew Pressman, FAIA, an architect, Professor Emeritus at the University of New Mexico, and Adjunct Professor at the University of Maryland, leads his own award-winning architectural firm in Washington, DC. He has written numerous critically acclaimed books and articles, and he holds a Master's degree from the Harvard University Graduate School of Design.

"Andrew Pressman's exemplary new book is an accessible, readable, and eminently usable introduction to design thinking. The book encourages individual experimentation and flexibility, empowering readers to make the design thinking process their own."

—Marilys R. Nepomechie, FAIA,
ACSA Distinguished Professor, Florida International University

DESIGN THINKING

A GUIDE TO CREATIVE PROBLEM SOLVING FOR EVERYONE

ANDREW PRESSMAN

Routledge
Taylor & Francis Group

LONDON AND NEW YORK

First published 2019
by Routledge
2 Park Square, Milton Park, Abingdon, Oxon OX14 4RN

and by Routledge
711 Third Avenue, New York, NY 10017

Routledge is an imprint of the Taylor & Francis Group, an informa business

© 2019 Andrew Pressman

British Library Cataloguing-in-Publication Data
A catalogue record for this book is available from the British Library

Library of Congress Cataloging-in-Publication Data
Names: Pressman, Andy, author.
Title: Design thinking : a guide to creative problem solving for everyone /
Andrew Pressman.
Description: New York : Routledge, 2019. | Includes bibliographical
references and index.
Identifiers: LCCN 2018026556 (print) | LCCN 2018027082 (ebook) |
ISBN 9781317202844 (pdf) | ISBN 9781317202837 (epub) | ISBN
9781317202820 (kindle) | ISBN 9781138673458 (hb : alk. paper) | ISBN
9781138673472 (pb : alk. paper) | ISBN 9781315561936 (ebook)
Subjects: LCSH: Problem solving. | Creative thinking.
Classification: LCC BF449 (ebook) | LCC BF449 .P74 2019 (print) | DDC
153.4/3—dc23
LC record available at https://lccn.loc.gov/2018026556

ISBN: 978-1-138-67345-8 (hbk)
ISBN: 978-1-138-67347-2 (pbk)
ISBN: 978-1-315-56193-6 (ebk)

Typeset in Galliard
by Swales & Willis Ltd, Exeter, Devon, UK

To Lisa who claims that she married me because I said, "Everything in life is a design problem—and a good architect can solve *any* design problem!"

CONTENTS

PART 1   Processes   1

1 DESIGN THINKING OVERVIEW | 3

2 BUILDING BLOCKS OF DESIGN THINKING | 13

3 TOOLS AND STRATEGIES | 51

PART 2 Applications   63

4 POLITICS AND SOCIETY | 65

5 BUSINESS | 81

6 HEALTH AND SCIENCE | 119

7 LAW | 129

8 WRITING | 139

FIGURES

interviews is very much analogous to the iterative process of design thinking | 116

6.1 Reframing questions can shed light on possible new directions toward finding a solution. For example, instead of: "Is there another, creative way of destroying or removing cancer cells?" we might ask, "What if there is a different, perhaps better means to achieve remission in a given case?" | 126

7.1 Whenever possible, present alternatives (together with their respective pros and cons) as a means to elicit discussion and to arrive at an even better solution | 135

FOREWORD

A ndrew Pressman's exemplary new book is an accessible, readable and eminently usable introduction to design thinking. For those in fields extending from the more traditionally creative to business, politics, medicine, and writing, the book illuminates the critical components of a professional skill set increasingly linked to leadership capacity, one whose perceived value grows daily. Unlike many how-to books, it avoids the prescriptive and formulaic. Instead, the book encourages individual experimentation and flexibility, empowering readers to make the design thinking process their own.

At the forefront of disciplinary discourse on effective professional practice and leadership, design thinking occupies a unique position. A process for creative problem solving and innovation, design thinking has come into its own over the past two decades, emerging as an invaluable tool—one whose effectiveness extends well beyond the disciplines traditionally linked to design practices. Increasingly, the solution-focused methods of design thinking are employed to address complex challenges that demand input from, and responsiveness to, a plurality of disciplinary knowledge, and a diversity of experience and perspective.

Well-researched, clearly organized, and cogently argued, the book unpacks and elucidates strategies for individual actors. Its numerous interviews and case studies probe for understanding, modeling the very investigative practices it recommends. As a result, the material speaks effectively and directly through the thoughtful voices of its protagonist experts, whose wide-ranging perspectives inform many of its most valuable insights.

Foregrounding the very human operation of creative problem solving at any scale, the book rewards the reader with awareness of a multi-track process at once empowering and inspirational. It describes a type of applied research that places communication and understanding at its center, one whose outcomes privilege the empathetic and responsive. A synthetic process focused on solutions, design thinking innovates as it reframes conundrums, breaks impasses, and dissolves knotty intricate challenges. Tolerant of ambiguity and risk, embracing failure as an opportunity for learning, successful design thinkers reconcile a diversity of perspectives, experiences and areas of expertise. They create and test prototypes through iterative loops, aspiring not to singular, but rather optimal solutions to problems.

Design thinking claims territory that lies someplace between the methods and cognitive time frames of science and art, incorporating key elements of each while forging its own. An increasingly valuable tool to address complexity in myriad disciplines, design thinking requires a specialized but attainable leadership skill set. That process is measurably facilitated by this excellent book.

Marilys R. Nepomechie, FAIA
ACSA Distinguished Professor

College of Communication, Architecture + the Arts

Florida International University

PREFACE

Design thinking is a powerful process that facilitates the understanding and framing of problems, enables creative solutions, and may provide fresh perspectives on our physical and social landscapes. Not just for architects or product developers, design thinking can be applied across many disciplines to solve real-world problems and reconcile dilemmas. It is a tool that may trigger inspiration and the imagination, and lead to innovative ideas that are responsive to the needs and issues of stakeholders.

Interpreting the process of design thinking and customizing it so that it will be personally relevant and useful for a unique set of circumstances is not easy. But the rewards of arriving at an excellent outcome, frequently in poetic fashion, cannot be overstated. *Design Thinking: A Guide to Creative Problem Solving for Everyone* will assist in addressing a full spectrum of challenges from the most vexing to the everyday.

This volume is conceived as a primer in design thinking to be immediately useful for a wide audience, and to support the now ubiquitous general education, business, and engineering courses in both college and graduate school curricula. *Design Thinking* is distinctive because it is directed primarily to individuals (as opposed to teams) without any prerequisites to help solve myriad problems that are *not* typically associated with design. Practicing professionals in the design and construction industry who want to rediscover the magic and delight of doing design—particularly with all the constraints and complexities inherent in a real-world context—should find the book refreshing and energizing as well.

So, what exactly is design thinking, and how is it distinct and different from other problem-solving approaches? Will the reader be able to understand the process sufficiently to apply it to help solve problems or work on projects more creatively? If so, how? Answers to these fundamental questions will be set forth clearly and succinctly in the chapters to follow.

Design Thinking: A Guide to Creative Problem Solving for Everyone is organized into two parts. The first part dives into the process itself, explicitly defining and describing design thinking, and then presenting and evaluating various strategies to cultivate it, which may ultimately provide breakthrough ideas. This is not intended to be a substitute for the expert judgment, knowledge, and experience of design professionals but rather it delineates a way of thinking that might prove quite useful for those who are not design professionals.

The second part of *Design Thinking: A Guide to Creative Problem Solving for Everyone* will illuminate the application of design thinking to diverse problems in several different realms not usually thought to be connected to design, such as politics and society, business, health and science, law, and writing. Elaboration of the design thinking process in Part 1 is informed by interviews conducted with select individuals in Part 2 who have practiced design thinking in some meaningful way to make a difference in their lives—and in the world. My hope is that the examples in Part 2 will be instructive, inspirational, and generalizable to readers' specific circumstances.

Design Thinking celebrates the absence of specific formulae, algorithms, or templates for design thinking. A formulaic, simplistic approach can severely limit creative possibilities for solving problems or even finding the right questions. The best process is inherently dynamic, changing in response to the nature of the situation and the individuals involved. A thorough analysis of the problem's context as well as of the stakeholders themselves, therefore, are critical components of design thinking. Moreover, because design thinking is a process, the ideas are scalable so as to address problems large and small.

Flexibility in solving different kinds of problems will be underscored. At the same time, analogies to an architect designing a building will be invoked throughout to illustrate components of the process in action, recognizing one of the venerable design professions from which design thinking has evolved. This acknowledges a certain foundational rigor and legitimacy. I would like to share two quotes from anonymous reviewers of the proposal for this book, each of whom supports this notion:

- The significance of this book is that it reclaims the design thinking discourse for architecture. It offers insight into the ways architects do design thinking and translates those ways of processing information and acting upon the world into a broad variety of contexts.

- As a popular guide to design thinking, this could be a useful contribution to the literature of 'demystified' thinking that comes out of codified professional knowledge.

In the design process, architects are routinely required to reconcile conflicts among various stakeholders who want more space, prefer certain aesthetic features, or demand the highest quality construction but have low budgets. The best architects are able to juggle and integrate the many variables, and use conflicts—or constraints—as the fuel that motivates great solutions. In other words, great architects are taught to create and focus order out of chaos and complexity. Why shouldn't professionals in other disciplines take advantage of this mindset?

I am a big fan of collaborative work (see *Designing Relationships: The Art of Collaboration in Architecture*, Routledge, 2014), but readers will not always have a team of people at their disposal to creatively solve an urgent problem. While teams could (and do) successfully embrace the processes shown herein, the focus in this book is on how design thinking can benefit individuals. There are places within the design-thinking loop where individuals can recruit others to help, for example, with criticism or ideation. The point I want to underscore, though, is that design thinking can be valuable to a large number of individuals, independent of any professional or personal affiliations.

Great architects typically question and transcend the building program given to them by clients in order to create something more meaningful and special than just solving the functional problem at hand. That's what design thinking can do for many types of problems, and should be considered one of its defining measures.

It is tempting to suggest that most challenges in life may be expressed as design problems and effectively managed as such. Solutions to even the most mundane problems can benefit from an infusion of purposeful creativity—derived from the seemingly magical perspective of design thinking.

Andrew Pressman, FAIA

Washington, DC

May 2018

ACKNOWLEDGMENTS

Francesca Ford, Publisher, Architecture was brilliant in helping me bounce the idea around for this book. Her flexibility to meet at The Boot at Sarratt, a pub conducive to innovative thinking (and proximate to WB studios and Harry Potter—the perfect venue), was very much appreciated. Moreover, Fran's editorial guidance and constructive and substantive suggestions were extremely helpful in developing the manuscript. I am indeed grateful for her ongoing support.

A big thank you to the entire Routledge production team including (but certainly not limited to) Trudy Varcianna (Senior Editorial Assistant), George Warburton (Editorial Manager at Swales & Willis), and Judith Harvey (copy-editing).

I am deeply indebted to Marilys Nepomechie for writing a powerful and articulate Foreword.

Sincere appreciation to the peer reviewers for their thoughtful criticism, which helped to shape and inform the content.

Special thanks to Michael Tardif and Mady Simon for their encouragement and passion about the value of design thinking, and for weighing-in on the subtitle.

I would like to acknowledge Peter Pressman for superior editorial acumen and incisive critiques.

The following individuals (in alphabetical order) graciously gave their time to be interviewed and contributed wonderful insights that significantly enrich this volume: James Barker, Victoria Beach, Mark Childs, Francesco Crocenzi, Charles Heuer, Mark Johnson, Meredith Kauffman, Bon Ku, Charles Linn, Scott Phillips, Diego Ruzzarin, Mady Simon, Richard Swett, Michael Tardif, and Jay Wickersham.

And, of course, much gratitude to Lisa, Samantha, and Daniel for providing sage advice and inspiration, as always.

Part 1

PROCESSES

Design thinking is a skill that may be difficult to acquire but is absolutely learnable. Once acquired, problems begin to look like design problems that *you* have the potential to solve creatively.

The design-thinking process is framed, clarified, placed in perspective, and thoroughly analyzed in Part 1. This first part sets forth a dynamic template for the process, which can itself be "designed" or customized as a function of a particular challenge. Here, the book begins to unravel some of the mystery and vagueness typically associated with design thinking by clearly examining the process as a whole; identifying and analyzing all the various building blocks or components of design thinking, and determining which components can best be applied or prioritized for a given situation, culminating in a comprehensive master plan that has been driven and shaped by design thinking.

It will be shown that the elements of design can be cherry-picked, refined, weighted, and combined into various hybrids, depending on the problem and its context, to yield a unique process for each problem. Running through a series of elements could be considered completion of a customized loop, which will produce new information and effective ideas—and may either crystallize a solution to a problem, or suggest new questions for yet another loop of inquiry, which will yield more synthetic insight and build on previous ideas.

Part 1 of *Design Thinking* will also elaborate on various tools and strategies that can nurture curiosity, exploration and discovery, and advance the design-thinking process to arrive at the optimal solutions to which I've been alluding. Insights will be offered to help support an open mind in order to further optimize potential as a design thinker.

I would emphasize several points that may become apparent and resonate with readers:

- Certain aspects of design thinking may already be familiar, natural, or even automatic for some. If this is the case, then you will have a great advantage in applying the process to the most challenging problems.

- The *process* of design thinking itself can and should be enjoyable, even exciting, in contrast to the ubiquitous, algorithmic, and often superficial goals of rapid gratification with an exclusive focus on self-serving deliverables.

- Consider engaging in design thinking as a full-bodied *investment* in the future of whatever endeavors the design thinker undertakes. Design thinking becomes less daunting and more efficient with an expanding fund of knowledge and experience.

Readers should note the special signposts where many specific design-thinking tactics described in Part 1 are showcased in actual real-life situations in Part 2. This is intended to expressly connect theory and practice.

1

DESIGN THINKING OVERVIEW

DEFINING DESIGN THINKING

There is no general agreement on a precise definition of design thinking; there are variations across disciplinary cultures, and different meanings depending on its context.[1] For example, design thinking in architecture is different from design thinking in a management context. The design process is dynamic, and can be complicated, messy, and nuanced as a function of specific realm and application. Moreover, there are additional layers of mystery associated with creativity itself, hence the challenge inherent in efforts to define it.

Notwithstanding the daunting qualifications noted above, it is imperative to develop a general sense of design thinking—a view from 35,000 feet—in order to set the stage for an explicit delineation of the specific components of the design process. First, here are some general thoughts—design thinking is:

- A process that results in a plan of action to improve a situation.

- A skill that incorporates situational awareness and empathy into idea generation.

- A tool that invokes analytical as well as creative thought to solve problems that consider context, stakeholder requirements and preferences, logistical issues, and cost.

- A mindset in which ideas are triggered from diverse, even discrepant, sources, and then built upon to inform progressively better solutions to challenges.

- A series of actions and an accumulation of provisional inputs that are structured by a loop in which problems are defined, research and analysis are conducted, and ideas are proposed and then subjected to critical feedback and modification, which in turn leads to repeating parts of the loop to further refine the ideas.

Personally, I would characterize design thinking as a fundamentally creative process that is driven by specific problems and individuals, yet transcends conventional or obvious solutions. While there is no magic formula, I would assert that the components of design thinking can be studied, systematically characterized, and rationally wedded to a process that yields effective and innovative solutions. Focusing and beginning to operationalize, it includes the following building blocks:

- **Information gathering**. Thoroughly research the context and stakeholders to arrive at a deep understanding of all relevant issues, conflicts, and constraints surrounding the problem. Examine historical perspectives, and a range of precedents that might be applicable to the problem. Conduct effective interviews, perform a mini-ethnography, and consult with key knowledgeable people to accelerate understanding. All of this data may provide a richer background that informs the design investigation and may trigger ideas.

- **Problem analysis and definition**. Rigorous analysis is necessary to ensure identification of the most salient problem, which may be masked because of an immediate acceptance of the problem at face value. Question the status quo; question initial assumptions and reframe the problem. Analysis is also a meaningful prerequisite for brainstorming; it results in a clear, orderly, and fine-grained view of the problem from multiple perspectives.

- **Idea generation**. Brainstorming and visioning sessions to create as many ideas—good, bad, and silly—as possible, informed by the information gathered to date together with the problem analysis. Consider and combine various influences to create innovative diagrammatic concepts or outlines of ideas.

- **Synthesis through modeling**. Take the best ideas to a higher degree of resolution and detail, resulting in several alternative prototypes, models, or draft solutions. These vehicles not only serve as good simulations of proposed preliminary solutions but, most importantly, can and should facilitate manipulation, experimentation, and even play. In all cases, regardless of success or failure, learning and discovery are paramount.

- **Critical evaluation**. With this essential step of testing the model, there is an opportunity to make the solution or project better; to validate (or not) concepts and solutions relative to the problem definition by subjecting them to critical appraisal from stakeholders, colleagues, and objective outsiders. Feedback from stakeholders is especially valuable to make meaningful revisions. Embrace constructive criticism from whatever source, make changes without diluting a strong idea, and test again.

Solutions should pass through the above loop of components as many times as appropriate to the problem (see Figure 1.1). In other words, get feedback, evaluate the outcomes, adjust the components, and

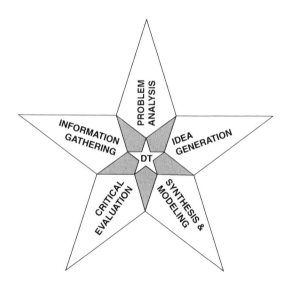

Figure 1.1 The fundamental building blocks of design thinking (DT) that together form a "loop." This diagram is intended to underscore the nonlinear nature of DT, and how the blocks may be interconnected and overlapped.

Source: The author.

repeat the loop with new data. Then implement. The clichés apply: nothing succeeds like a try, and nothing succeeds like a response to the most recent failure.

How is design thinking distinct and different from other problem-solving approaches?

Design thinking is *not* an algorithm; unlike math and science problems, there is no single, right, absolute answer; there are multiple solutions, some perhaps more optimal than others. Indeed, design thinking—especially learning about problems through analyzing context and stakeholders—is closely aligned with social science thinking. Likewise, journalistic approaches to gathering information[2]— a very important first step—is integral to design thinking. Peter Merholz makes the point that design thinking can be a great complement to other disciplinary ways of approaching problems, bringing a diversity of perspectives to bear to solve complex problems.[3]

The process of design thinking may be disruptive in a most constructive fashion. When a potential design solution is evaluated, it may actually lead to a change in the initial question, or even to a significant modification or rejection of the original hypothesis. The term "disruptive technologies" is attributed to Clayton M. Christensen and Joseph Bower who used it in their 1995 *Harvard Business Review* article titled, "Disruptive Technologies: Catching the Wave." Since then, the term has evolved to include any innovation that disrupts conventional models. Disruption, then, is one element that fundamentally distinguishes design thinking from straight hypothesis testing or conventional research.

CUSTOMIZING THE PROCESS

A prescriptive how-to "step-by-step" approach to design thinking, while useful in some situations, may be flawed by oversimplifying or by positing rigid algorithms. These pitfalls may discourage or suppress innovation, unique personal perspectives, and nuances. So, before jumping into the work, consider the degree to which each of the building blocks summarized in the section above (and detailed in the next chapter) are applicable.

The building blocks are dynamic and can be cherry-picked, modified, prioritized, and choreographed into various hybrids and amalgamations (see Figures 1.2, 1.3, and 1.4). Take cues from the specific circumstances of the problem—the stakeholders, context, and the nature of the problem itself—to yield a unique design thinking method for each situation. A fresh gestalt arises with each and every project, which is one reason that design thinking is so fascinating and exciting. *The process can be just as creative and unique as the outcome*. Keep your eyes open and free your imagination in response to the challenge at hand.

A design-thinking master plan for a particular problem can be developed as a general guide or template. Certainly there will be variations in focus, content, and sequence of steps as a function of personal and project idiosyncrasies, and some steps may even be skipped or combined. For example, the information gathering and problem analysis and definition blocks may be merged, condensed, or omitted entirely when there is already a reasonable familiarity with the problem, its background, and surrounding issues (see Figure 1.2).

Another scenario could imply that the idea generation and synthesis through modeling blocks should be intertwined. If the deliverable is a written proposal or business plan, for example, writing a draft and producing a final document (prototype) are all part of the same, continuous effort. It makes no sense to have an artificial boundary, especially when individual work habits are so variable (see Figure 1.3).

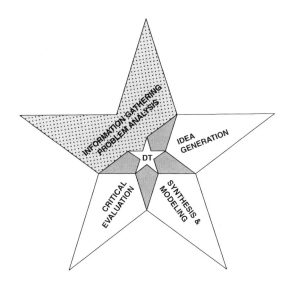

Figure 1.2 The information-gathering and problem-analysis blocks (gray with dots) may be merged, condensed, or omitted entirely when there is a reasonable familiarity with aspects of the problem, its background, and surrounding issues.

Source: The author.

Expanding the idea-generation block to include representative stakeholders by conducting a special workshop or "charrette" is a potential opportunity to advance the work (see Figure 1.4). As an added benefit, this strategy may also *incorporate* the information-gathering and problem-analysis blocks by diving into the "design" work at the start. It launches ideation as a means to fully grasp all the issues and salient factors; to elicit more information and develop detailed, relevant questions; and to test preliminary ideas and an overarching vision for the solution—and to receive immediate feedback on which to base further investigations.

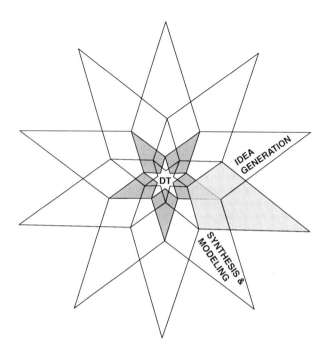

Figure 1.3 Depending on the specific challenge and individual work habits, some building blocks may be intertwined as part of a continuous effort, for example, idea generation and synthesis and modeling (light gray).

Source: The author.

Charrette is a term used to describe a process technique to jump-start creative design thinking, usually at the beginning of a project, and involves a total immersion in brainstorming investigations in a very compressed, uninterrupted time frame, either independently or in a team context. This strategy can be extremely effective, even inspiring, in identifying key issues and as a starting point for meaningful in-depth discussions with stakeholders.

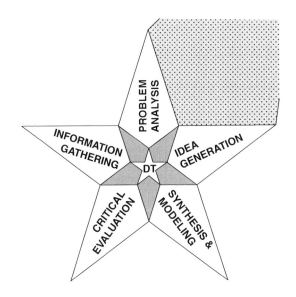

Figure 1.4 Expanding blocks, such as problem analysis and idea generation, to include representative stakeholders (gray with dots) may be an opportunity to enrich the process as a function of the unique problem circumstances.

Source: The author.

A slightly different way of imagining the design-thinking process is described by Tim Brown, head of IDEO, an innovation and design firm in Palo Alto. He says: "The design process is best described metaphorically as a system of spaces rather than a predefined series of orderly steps." Brown tags the spaces as follows: (1) *Inspiration*—for the circumstances (i.e., problems, opportunities) that motivate the search for solutions; (2) *ideation*—for the process of generating, developing, and testing ideas that may lead to solutions; and (3) *implementation*—for the charting of a path to market (or to wherever or however the solution is manifest).[4] Just as with the iterative loops described earlier, as work evolves, it passes through the first two "spaces" multiple times.

In contrast to a rigid formula for design thinking, creating a diagrammatic framework (as exemplified in Figures 1.2, 1.3, and 1.4) for engaging a specific problem provides guidance while promoting flexibility—and suggests an optimal, customized design-thinking process—based upon unique individual and problem circumstances.

NOTES

1 Ulla Johansson-Sköldberg, Jill Woodilla, and Mehaves Çetinkaya, "Design Thinking: Past, Present and Possible Futures," *Creativity and Innovation Management*, vol. 22, no. 2, 2013, p. 121.

2 Peter Merholz, "Why Design Thinking Won't Save You," *Harvard Business Review Blog Network*, October 9, 2009.

3 Ibid.

4 Tim Brown, "Design Thinking," *Harvard Business Review*, vol. 86, no. 6, June 2008, pp. 88–89.

2

BUILDING BLOCKS OF DESIGN THINKING

INFORMATION GATHERING

Design thinking begins with an immersion in the unique circumstances of the problem. It is a process of discovery in which clues to the solution may become evident as the issues are explored fully and deeply from multiple perspectives.

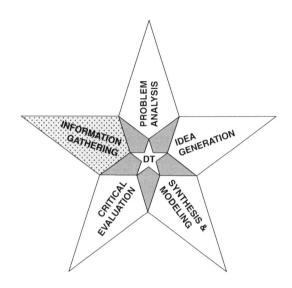

Empathy

Borrowing from anthropology, conducting an abbreviated and customized form of qualitative research—ethnography—or what Clifford Geertz described as "thick description,"[1] is a way to become immersed in a problem and go beyond a superficial understanding. In an increasingly high-tech and sterile world, spending time with, effectively observing, and interacting with stakeholders in their natural surroundings can reveal much about the relevant issues, illuminate motivations, provide insight about underlying positions, and generate ideas about solutions. Conducting an effective focused interview is a fabulous tool for this type of information gathering, and is a very valuable and surprisingly undervalued component of the design thinking process.

An alternative or adjunct to the interview is to enlist an expert who can provide a briefing on the issues and thus accelerate understanding of

> If, however, you can go beyond overt conscious wants and delve into what really drives, excites, and motivates a person, group, or company, then you can begin to propose solutions that are enlightening, wonderful, and cost-effective.

the problem. However, there is really no substitute for a first-hand participant-observation perspective, which can facilitate "an emotional connection to a problem, and with that connection comes insight."[2] Madlen Simon, a professor at the University of Maryland who teaches a course on design thinking, neatly underscores this point below:

> See Chapter 5 Business > Empathy as a means to innovate in a pharmaceutical company.

> We often don't know the people who matter in our interactions. That's valuable in order to acquire knowledge that is relevant and important. Therefore, it is great to have a toolkit of skills for learning how to better understand people. People always have to be involved. The concept of immersing yourself in another person's environment and situation—asking probing questions at a minimum—is essential.[3]

Because stakeholders often have difficulty in articulating needs and problems, there is an opportunity to be a creative diagnostician in the design-thinking process. Moreover, if you simply accept a problem at face value, you can only deliver a solution to that problem. If, however, you can go beyond overt conscious wants and delve into what really drives, excites, and motivates a person, group, or company, then you can begin to propose solutions that are enlightening, wonderful, and cost-effective. *The universe starts to open up once you get inside the minds of people or groups.*[4] One of the great attributes of design thinking is this ability to transcend the pragmatic and do more than merely solve a *given* problem.

As noted, a principal tool of engagement is the interview. Below are some tips to facilitate a great interview.

■ **Do your homework**. Preparation is critical. Take some time before an initial meeting to form some specific hypotheses about the issues, hopes, and dreams. Utilize these notions to shape initial questioning either to confirm or reject your ideas. In addition, have questions in the event the conversation starts to fade. Learn something about the interviewee or the interviewee's perspectives that will jump-start the conversation and put the interviewee sufficiently at ease to open up and set a relaxed tone.

■ **Establish rapport**. Share your own story and listen to their story. Be yourself; get personal—share your vision of the problem; you should neither affect some wooden formality nor be excessively casual and familiar. Cultivate a respectful alliance. The stakeholder's perception that at some level he or she is cared for or taken seriously will likely enhance participation, the quality and depth of information offered, and ensure wishes are voiced. Acknowledge and appreciate the stakeholders' unique perspectives, especially if different from your own. *Put yourself in the interviewee's shoes*. At this early stage, maintaining an open mind and low-profile ego will enhance truly reciprocal communication, and promote rapport. In other words, model the behavior you want others to emulate.

■ **Listen actively and carefully**. Empathy will help you to figure out the interests and motivations of the stakeholders. Active listening means fully understanding and actually processing all that is being said by focusing complete attention on the speaker and testing and amplifying what they communicate. Discover the value of what is being said between the lines, then check it out with follow-up questioning. Test any new hypotheses by simply asking if they make sense. Paraphrase responses to your questions to invite clarification, correction, and additional detail. Repeat key words or phrases, again to invite clarification and elaboration.

> See Chapter 5 Business > Visioning, listening, and diagramming at a university > Listening.

- *Formulate thoughtful, probing questions*. From the initial questioning, confirmation of hypotheses allows you the luxury of eliciting valuable details, or, conversely, rejection of expectations should immediately set up questions designed to discover new facts that will in turn support alternative ideas. Be genuinely curious, and remember the goal is to keep learning even if you believe the responses to a given question may not at all illuminate what you're exploring. Dig deeply after a response. For example, ask: Why did you do that? How did it work out for you? How do you feel? What did you expect? Be curious and care, but be careful not to be confrontational as that may impede forthright responses.

- *Observe sensitively and with focus*. This applies especially when you have the opportunity to engage an interviewee in the environment in which the problem or challenge is situated. A first-hand experience can be very revealing and contribute to a deep understanding, particularly to an outsider who can be objective (see context analysis in the next section for more information). Note body language, mannerisms, facial expressions, emotional state, and even taste in clothing. Consider the details of the surrounding environment: what do furnishings, artifacts on the desk, and photos or images on the wall say about the person or the problem? Is the person organized or messy? Respond sympathetically even if you don't necessarily agree; convey that what is being said is important to you.

- **Maintain a sense of humor**. This can be a terrific strategy to successfully establish rapport and engage stakeholders. Steve Martin's[5] observation of Carl Reiner as a film director is a great model: "He had an entrenched sense of glee; he used humor as a gentle way of speaking difficult truths; and he could be effortlessly frank."

- **And, avoid the following**. (1) The temptation to interrupt; you could miss an important comment or nuance. (2) Questions that result in yes or no responses. (3) Leading questions that consciously or unconsciously elicit the response you want to hear—try not to manipulate the interviewee. (4) Writing or referring to notes or an iPad screen. Writing while someone is taking the time to talk with you may be experienced as distancing or rude, so take notes privately; reflect and record impressions after the interview. Likewise, reading questions can disrupt the flow of the conversation. Prepare questions, as previously noted, but as a way of imprinting background information rather than for explicit reading.

Ask questions about what people want—and what they don't want. Review the problem issues and elicit suggestions for improving or detailing them; probe to discover the unstated problems.

> See Chapter 5 Business > Dinner conversation as a model for effective interviews.

Much tangential information is bound to result from responses to questions and conversations with stakeholders. Use some open-ended questions, but give gentle direction to help keep focus on the issue at hand (i.e., "I'd like to hear more about that, but I was particularly intrigued by what you started to say about ..."). Try to avoid preoccupation with irrelevant factors, however colorful they may be. Keep the big picture in clear focus. And remain alert to valuable bits of information that may spontaneously emerge as something unexpected, which could be a clue to a possible solution.

So, embrace and celebrate the unforeseen! You may find that an interviewee is a bit quirky, illogical, or even somewhat crazy. This is not necessarily a bad thing because a very diverse range of people can trigger some of the most creative and innovative ideas.

Empower the stakeholders to meaningfully contribute to the solution. During interviews, keep in mind that it may be helpful to identify and formally recognize select stakeholders as collaborators who could enrich an idea-generation workshop or brainstorming session later in the process. Professor Simon weighs-in on interviewing with this astute comment.

> See Chapter 4 Politics and society > Expanding the politics of civic engagement > Writing and passing the Congressional Accountability Act.

What you're really looking for in addition to the facts is the emotions. If you can put up sensitive antennae and listen for emotional shifts in the conversation, you can begin to know when you've touched on something that the person you're interviewing feels deeply about. And if you can make a connection with their emotions, chances are you can design something that's going to please them in a meaningful way. That's one of the places where great solutions to problems come from: creating things that people feel emotionally connected to.[6]

Empathy and travel

Madlen Simon offers a distinctive application of design thinking:

> Design thinking has enhanced my travel experiences. Now
> that I'm armed with empathy skills, I find that I'm much more
> able to reach out to people; to start conversations and learn a
> lot more about the place I'm visiting, rather than just walking
> around by myself. I'm really trying to see places through other
> people's eyes—that's an incredible way to enrich the travel
> experience.[7]

It is interesting to note that the same empathic skills used for
interviewing can cross over to other endeavors. For example, Mark
Johnson, as marketing manager for a building product manufacturer,
stated, "I learned quickly that the coaching and mentoring skills
needed for success were based largely on listening, watching, and
focusing on individual motivations."[8]

Precedents

Invoking ideas from the past—analyzing, understanding, and interpreting them—can inspire design solutions in the present and for the
future. The underlying principles revealed in an analysis of a relevant
precedent—a previous solution to a similar problem that could be
used as an example—may have significant value in the discovery or
ideation phase of design thinking.

However, since every (design) problem is unique, blindly copying
solutions from the past is fraught with risk and superficiality.
Emerson famously claimed: "The imitator dooms himself to hope-
less mediocrity."[9] If there is no critical thinking, it is all too easy to
extract the wrong lessons, especially if the context and specific
circumstances surrounding the problem are not fully considered.

So, use the great idea but tweak and purposefully apply it; *build on it and make it better*.

So, use the great idea but tweak and purposefully apply it; *build on it and make it better*.

There is benefit to searching for, and becoming informed about, similar problems and their solutions—even if the solutions are mundane. It assists in getting up to speed with "cookbook" solutions, which can then jump-start thinking in creative ways in relation to a different set of conditions. This knowledge base can save time by obviating the need to reinvent the wheel. Moreover, diving deeply into the issues surrounding a similar challenge can help to illuminate all facets of the present problem.

> See Chapter 5 Business > Creativity in the culinary arts.

Another perspective involves applying precedents from apparently unrelated areas to solving a problem. Examining alternative ideas that may seem far afield and exploring how those insights might be incorporated in a solution to the current problem could yield a potentially exciting and fresh "design" response. Architects do this all the time: for example, recalling the way a roof structure was configured or the way materials or natural light were manipulated on a building visited while traveling and documented in a journal can help to generate a creative concept for a new project.

> See Chapter 6 Health and science > A design approach to treating cancer.

Peter Rowe, in his seminal book on design thinking, underscores the point that analogies to ideas in other realms can serve a designer's purpose and become part of a repertoire of ideas that can be mined for different projects in the future.[10] For example, overlapping fish scales were the inspiration for the design of body armor that has typically conflicting characteristics of being both protective and flexible.[11] This is a brilliant engineering solution arising from a precedent from nature. Imitate! And apply the idea in a new way.

Context

Context includes all the relevant influences shaping a problem, from environmental variables (physical constraints) to social, cultural, and historical factors (stakeholder requirements and preferences). The systematic investigation of all of these conditions contributes to a solid foundation for design thinking—and connects the problem to the local setting, the neighborhood, and the larger community. While collecting this data may at first seem tedious and unimaginative, it can be an avenue, or, indeed, the point of departure for an exciting resolution.

Context is important because of its contribution to making a problem unique and circumstance-specific. The best solutions are informed by the context, and are certainly not developed in isolation. Appreciating the context helps to develop perspective and its underpinnings, to anticipate challenges on the path to solutions, and to create more effective and sensitive design responses. Without contextual knowledge, assumptions about possible solutions could be way off base. *A good idea in one context may not be good at all in another*.

One strategy for fully evoking and understanding context is to be a detective: observe. Every situation possesses a unique mosaic of attributes and external forces that must be identified, integrated, and interpreted. Begin with listing and describing them and then record observations both objectively and impressionistically. Define what it is about the context that drives the possibilities and challenges of the solution.

If applicable, determine the social factors that may influence the project. Identify and then solicit opinions from stakeholders and influential people who may only be tangentially connected with the issue at hand. Ask about pressing problems and political exigencies; ask what might be done to maximize community support if appropriate. Sensitivity to all this potential input will help to promote the ultimate success of a project or solution to a problem, as stakeholders will feel somewhat invested knowing their feedback has been acknowledged.

PROBLEM ANALYSIS AND DEFINITION

This may seem counterintuitive, but defining the right problem may actually be a creative act. Even if a problem is not fully articulated, it may be useful to forge ahead and work through the design-thinking loop with incomplete data as a means to further delineate and amplify the issues. This is another great attribute of design thinking. Other conventional problem-solving techniques suggest that there must be a clear problem formulation before taking action to solve it. With design thinking, however, continuing dialogues, diagnoses, and reframing of the problem throughout the process ensure an optimal solution.

See Chapter 7 Law > Problem definition.

> Never accept problems at face value—always challenge them to either
> affirm their validity or recast them after further investigation.

Never accept problems at face value—always challenge them to either affirm their validity or recast them after further investigation. While we want to be very sensitive to what stakeholders—clients or consumers or patients—tell us, we must be cautious about accepting their highly biased reports, and also their conclusions about what it all means and what they think is the best response. The real problem may be masked for a variety of reasons; it is easy to be misled by a less serious problem or a symptom. Take time to periodically review and reflect on all the information gathered from interviews and conversations with stakeholders, all aspects of the context, precedent searches, and any other

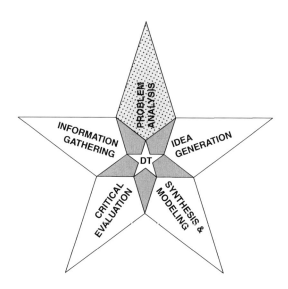

relevant sources. A main objective is to develop a deep, objective, and evidence-based understanding of the issues, constraints, challenges, and possibilities surrounding the problem along with its root causes.

> See Chapter 5 Business > Implementing a strategic technology plan > Reimagining electronic information exchange at construction handover.

Defining the right problem requires asking the right questions. *If the problem is framed too narrowly, it could limit an effective—much less an innovative—solution*. For example, in the 1960s, IBM was seeking the answer to a key question: "If a more reliable, cheaper, and faster process for photocopying were available, how many more copies would people make in a given year?" The problem was framed too narrowly as "copies from originals," rather than considering a potentially much larger market that included "copies of copies of copies." There was a big missed opportunity that might have been anticipated if the right questions were asked.[12] Avoiding the status quo and business as usual—even in asking initial questions about the problem—is an important part of the design-thinking mindset.

> See Chapter 4 Politics and society > Managing gridlocked debates > Flanders mansion.

> See Chapter 8 Writing > Draft as prototype.

Analyze, organize, visualize, and quantify the information collected in a way that helps to clearly articulate the essence of the problem, or at least have a working definition of the problem as it evolves. Consider the following tasks as a prerequisite to idea generation:

- Document specific and frequently expressed points or note-worthy comments from interviews with stakeholders, emphasizing different sides of the problem or illuminating some aspect of the problem.

- Identify areas for further research to complement the interviews.

- Develop lists, diagrams, and images highlighting key context observations; graphics can render lots of complex material in a way that is far more readily understood and interpreted.

- Formulate new questions related to the validity of the initial problem statement.

- Note any novel or unexpected patterns, relationships, or insights that may be evident.

- Eliminate the mass of extraneous material (carefully).

- Uncover the fundamental causes of the problem.

- Collapse a seemingly overwhelming problem into smaller, more manageable components (but keep the big picture in mind).

- Filter the relevant information into two categories for complex problems—general and specific. This will facilitate initial idea generation by not overloading that phase of the process with too much information at one time.

- Set forth the scope of the problem including constraints, concerns, and challenges; also include the ultimate objectives, hopes, and dreams (and their rationale). This could be considered the design criteria on which proposed solutions are evaluated.

Analysis is essential to set the stage for the most meaningful idea-generation session. Effective brainstorming can begin with a multidimensional and coherent understanding of the problem and its context from different points of view.

IDEA GENERATION

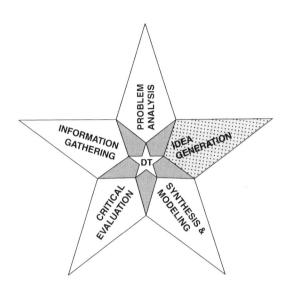

"Your conscience shouts, 'Here's what you should do,' while your intuition whispers, 'Here's what you could do.' Listen to that voice that tells you what you could do. Nothing will define your character more than that"—Steven Spielberg.[13]

Now that much information about the problem, stakeholders, and context has been elicited, researched, and analyzed—and all that knowledge internalized—the real fun begins. One thing to keep in mind is that objectively and narrowly responding to this input—while absolutely necessary—will only take you so far. It is time for getting loose; allowing an infusion of imagination, epiphany, innovation, and creativity; interpreting information and *merging it with your own creativity* into a meaningful solution.

See Chapter 4 Politics and society > Expanding the politics of civic engagement > Writing and passing the Congressional Accountability Act.

There are likely to be conflicting perspectives and hopes for certain outcomes as a function of the priorities of multiple stakeholders in any given problem. It behooves the design thinker to be as objective and responsive as possible to those priorities with one caveat: the personal traits, background, experience, intuition, and unique vision of you, the designer, should be acknowledged. It is important to be open to the ideas of others while at the same time committing to one's own ideals and impulses. This sounds like an inherent contradiction. Is it more courageous to listen and respond only to stakeholders, or to stubbornly stand behind some personalized ideal solution? Perhaps it is the tension between the practical and the ideal that motivates innovation and keeps creativity tied to the solution of mundane but often significant challenges.

Brainstorming

Typically thought of as a creative activity in a team context, the idea generation component of design thinking can also be very effective for individuals. Collaboration is great[14] but it is not always possible (nor desirable) to assemble a team to solve a problem. That said, it may be useful to recruit others to critique and comment as a way to capture diverse input and reap the benefits of collaborative work (see Critical evaluation, later in this chapter).

Brainstorming has been successfully deployed in some form for many years across numerous professions, industries, and businesses. Building on the ideas of Alex Osborn, who first outlined the principles of brainstorming in 1939,[15] below are a few of the basics that are essential to design thinking:

Work hard to mitigate the natural tendency that we all have to constantly evaluate.

- **Do not initially criticize or judge your ideas**. Evaluation should occur *after* the session and not while brainstorming is in process, otherwise you risk becoming frozen and kernels of potentially novel ideas will not have a chance to be developed. Work hard to mitigate the natural tendency that we all have to constantly evaluate.

- **Generate unfettered, wild, and crazy ideas**. In addition to generating the usual array of standard, expected, or obvious solutions, this strategy has a greater probability of leading to a solution that is innovative and creative. Here is where the now clichéd colorful Post-its, index cards, sketches and diagrams—filled with ideas—take center stage.

See Chapter 6 Health and science > Health care delivery.

- **Try to develop as many ideas as possible**. The more ideas that are on the table—flawed or not—the better chance to trigger something special and excellent. Perfection is not the goal; at this stage, sheer quantity is. Experiment. Do not wait for the lightning bolt of inspiration to strike.

- **Combine and build upon ideas**. Synthesizing or improving upon preliminary ideas that have been proposed should be part of the natural progression of a brainstorming session. Subdivide the ideas, organize, prioritize, or categorize them as a way to focus on a particular aspect of the problem (for example, attach Post-its under "big picture" and "specifics" headings, or place ideas into different information baskets). Coalesce the best

> Do not underestimate the value of having fun as an integral part of idea generation.

elements from many ideas into a completely new idea. Mark Johnson affirms the clear benefits of this element of design thinking: "We found each experiment to reinvent our [building product] business process often led to another innovative idea."[16]

At regular intervals, or after a brainstorming session, *reflect* and take stock: summarize important points, ideas, features, etc. Compare those to the overarching objectives that were outlined in the problem definition to ensure that the process is proceeding on the right track.

Design thinking attitude

The importance of approaching the ideation phase of design thinking with the right attitude cannot be emphasized enough. Do not underestimate the value of having fun as an integral part of idea generation. It helps to diffuse tension and stress, making it easier to loosen up and unlock creativity, and examine problems in many different ways. If the work is viewed as play then it is easier to brainstorm: free associate, turn ideas upside down and sideways, generate ideas quickly without caring about failure or criticism, and simply keep the work flowing. Learn to overcome inhibitions acquired through years of adulthood. Be mindful to do the following:

See Chapter 8 Writing > Draft as prototype.

■ **Embrace ambiguity**. There are bound to be many unknowns. New information may be brought to bear after work is initiated. Expect feedback from preliminary ideas to inform further development.

An optimal solution is more realistic than seeking one that is perfect.

See Chapter 5 Business > Implementing a strategic technology plan > Eureka moments and intuitive leaps.

In the search for that 'Eureka!' moment of a great design solution, we must often follow unclear instincts, fuzzy clues, or paths that seem to hold no promise. Yet, it is through this ambiguous terrain that we come to find our best solutions.[17]

See Chapter 8 Writing > Draft as prototype.

▪ *Have confidence in design thinking and your own instincts*. Be aware that there will always be a certain amount of insecurity or anxiety in the beginning of a project in which the outcome is unknown; assume that, with perseverance, there will be a successful result. Understand that initial ideas—especially those that are new or innovative—are especially delicate.

See Chapter 6 Health and science > A design approach to treating cancer.

Alternative solutions

An optimal solution is more realistic than seeking one that is perfect. There is a common misperception that perfection should be the overarching goal. Indeed, there is no single right answer or perfect solution to most problems; there are shades of gray—alternatives, with varying tradeoffs. Usually, one of those alternatives is the most promising. The optimal solution successfully addresses the highest priority objectives and/or satisfies most of the constraints and stakeholder wishes—in addition to providing the "goose bump factor" (see description below).

An outcome of idea generation should be several very different alternative schemes that address the issues outlined in the problem definition and its analysis. If one idea is rejected for whatever reason, then there are ten other very good ones to propose. If there is an obsession with creating the single perfect solution, you are more likely to end up frozen with the inability to imagine any other viable potential solutions.

See Chapter 7 Law > Alternatives and the big idea.

Baby steps

If at first things seem overwhelming, just chip away one bit at a time. If appropriate, temporarily eliminate minor details so attention can be focused on major elements only. This strategy is similar to computational thinking, which is defined in part as "using abstraction and decomposition when attacking a large complex task or designing a large complex system. It is separation of concerns."[18]

See Chapter 8 Writing > Writing prose for writing pros > Design thinking as rolling the snowball downhill.

Typically, at project or problem inception, there are so many variables to consider that it is practically impossible—or too daunting—to work with all of them at once. One strategy is to take baby steps in order to break down the problem into manageable pieces—let some of the constraints float for a while and work on other constraints. Go back and forth. One investigation informs the other. Another strategy is to consider the analogy to a jigsaw puzzle where you work on one piece at a time as a means to arriving at the complete picture. Moving back and forth between pieces here as well, while they are still being developed, can be very effective.

> See Chapter 5 Business > Implementing a strategic technology plan > Strategic plan as jigsaw puzzle.

Brainstorming tips

Below are some strategies to facilitate idea generation. Some will be more worthwhile than others as a function of the specific problem—and your personal style and proclivities.

- **Withhold judgment**. If you are constantly evaluating ideas, then some potentially great solutions may be missed. Fight against the natural inclination to erase or delete; archive the work—you may want to revisit an idea after some time and further explorations, to see it in a new light.

- **Focus the brainstorming sessions**. They can be dedicated to working on an aspect of the problem, the design of the process itself for solving the problem, or the big picture.

- **Engage in trial, error, and refinement**. This old dictum is a fine strategy for stimulating creativity. Sometimes you just need an arbitrary starting point from which to jump in, with the caveat that, for the most part, design decisions should be accountable. So, take action; that provides a basis for further exploration, and eventually, evaluation.

- **_Become immersed in the circumstances of the problem_**. Ideas will emerge and become evident the deeper you go and the more fully the issues are understood.

- **_Do something different; take a risk_**. Commit to the idea of discovery and innovation within the circumstances of the problem. Try changing the way you work to foster creativity. There is little growth or learning without risk.

- **_Bad ideas and failure are essential_**. Bad ideas are great because they often trigger exceptional ideas. The bad idea must be appreciated; that is, all ideas need to be considered (as noted above), nurtured, then rejected, accepted, or built upon—not immediately crushed. Acknowledge unsuccessful work as a valuable part of design thinking, and as an opportunity to learn, discover valuable information, and as motivation to innovate. The IDEO mantra, now a cliché, "Fail often to succeed sooner"[19] is particularly salient. Failure is so important on the road to innovation and success that a new museum—the Museum of Failure—recently opened in Sweden. It showcases high-profile failures such as the Bic for Her pen, Harley-Davidson perfume, and Colgate Beef Lasagna. According to Dr. Samuel West, an organizational psychologist and the museum's curator,

See Chapter 5 Business > Fast-fail and iterative.

The purpose of the museum is to show that innovation requires failure; if you are afraid of failure, then we can't innovate . . . if you're creating something new, you're going to fail. Don't be ashamed of it. Let's learn from these failures instead of ignoring them.[20]

- **View constraints as opportunities rather than as a limitation**. With a bit of creativity, problems can be transformed into unique assets. For example, in a renovation there is an existing structural column in the middle of an important space that seemingly disrupts the space. Instead of a costly removal, consider making it an integral part of the larger three-dimensional composition by adding another (nonstructural) matching column to create a gateway, or delineate a circulation path, or create a support core. Keep an open mind to new possibilities. Constraints are great because they force you to get more creative to arrive at a worthy solution. Remember to recognize the genuine opportunities as well.

- **Take the time to play "what if."** Develop a series of questions about what might be possible. Then consider the consequences, but do not worry about the answers right away. "If I do x then y or z happens," or, "if I do x then I have to address y set of problems." Be wary of the trap wherein it becomes so enjoyable to pose the questions that you don't get around to speculating about the answers (academic architects in particular are subject to this phenomenon). Here is a great snippet illustrating the "what if" game from architect Don Metz:

See Chapter 6 Health and science > A design approach to treating cancer.

As always, the process consists of questions built upon questions: What if? If this goes here, will this fit there? What is the appropriate hierarchy between this sequence of rooms? What are the sight lines and sources of light inside the house? What are the views from inside to outside—and from outside to inside? If I arrange the bedrooms at opposite ends of the house instead of above or below, how would that alter the client's expectations of interior zoning? Are there ways to profitably impose or disrupt a rhythm of elements (windows, doors, posts, beams, corners, casework, stairs), expand a space, or condense it down? Can I gain a sense of openness by letting a wall stop short of a ceiling—and still retain a sense of privacy? Some ideas begin to suggest others, some lead nowhere. As I prove and disprove each thesis, the search will lead to something that may work. Or not.[21]

The questions Metz poses to himself (above) become the primary means to stimulate creative responses.

▣ **Be passionate**. Look for some special element in the problem that has a personal connection on some dimension, which can activate something in your own soul and move you to express that in a way that substantively contributes to a potential solution.

▣ ***Assume your solution will be implemented***. This kind of mindset will help to realize a self-fulfilling prophecy, and will ensure your personal investment, which is so important in design thinking. Create your own brand of virtual reality by imagining yourself as each type of stakeholder and how they would specifically experience the solution or project. In this fashion, visualize your design solution and see it come to life, complete with all its benefits and problems.

See Chapter 5 Business > Visioning, listening, and diagramming at a university > Visioning.

- **Use words to facilitate idea generation**. Words that are intentionally vague allow for flexibility in interpretation, thus helping to spark new ideas. For example, what images come to mind when you reflect on words such as cluster, leverage, promote, layer, screen, and intersect? Another way to use words is to create a narrative vision of what a proposed solution might be like. Design the story surrounding the problem and solution— imagine different scenarios including events, mixes of people, and times.

See Chapter 8 Writing > Writing prose for writing pros > Getting to the aha moment.

- **Work in multiple scales simultaneously**. Take a step back; zoom out and zoom in. This can be beneficial because it ensures that the big picture is always in mind while not sacrificing attention to detail.

Typical mistakes in brainstorming

Below are some typical pitfalls to be recognized and avoided. In accordance with the cliché, these are easy to say, not so easy to do. But being aware of them can help with design thinking.

- **Responding to criticism is regarded as compromising design intent**. With a different attitude, revising a proposed solution can also be viewed as a chance to do more brainstorming, and make the solution or project even better.

- **An initial idea that is perceived as excellent should be carried through, completely intact, to the final outcome**. Related to an obsession with finding *the* perfect solution, infatuation with an idea should not get in the way of larger goals or the big picture. Openness to alternatives (perhaps equally infatuating but

> No single aspect or feature of a solution should be considered
> precious.

very different) is a hallmark of experience. Caveat: in some rare cases, a great, substantive initial idea may be worth fighting for.

- **The tail wagging the dog**. No single aspect or feature of a solution should be considered precious. Do not let an impressive detail dominate all decision-making.

- **Brainstorming resulted in lots of great ideas; let's use them all**. In general, when too many things are happening simultaneously, there is no one strong point of view. Do not dilute a good solid concept with a constellation of clever gestures. Albert Einstein said, "Any intelligent fool can make things bigger and more complex. It takes a touch of genius— and a lot of courage—to move in the opposite direction."

- **Working on tasks that do not thoughtfully advance the work**. Time is one of the most important resources we have. Mismanaging time by working on tasks that are interesting but only tangentially related to the problem is a common occurrence. Constantly monitor what you are doing to ensure that you don't get mired in inconsequential activities.

- **Keep revising a bad idea to make it work**. If it appears that too much revision is required, it may make sense to abandon the idea and start on a fresh alternative.

The goose bump factor

One feature that distinguishes design thinking is striving to integrate some sort of magical element, a critical intangible that separates a competent solution from a great one. Not all problems are amenable to this, but always look for opportunities to transcend solving the practical problem. Honor the problem but also create something beyond the immediate utility of the solution; perhaps something that the stakeholders might never have imagined. Reach for the greatest potential within the constraints, hopefully eliciting an emotional response. This represents design thinking at its best.

All the "dos and don'ts" in the preceding discussion may seem self-evident and may in fact be natural and automatic for some, but it is metaphorically worth rediscovering the wheel on occasion as we engage what appear to be more challenging problems as society becomes increasingly complex and also full of constraints—economic, regulatory, and ideologic. The reality is that it is more difficult to be creative and effective these days, so design thinking may well be more relevant than ever.

See Chapter 8 Writing > Draft as prototype.

SYNTHESIS THROUGH MODELING

If I can make it there
I'll make it anywhere.

Theme from *New York, New York*, composed by John Kander with lyrics by Fred Ebb, 1977.[22]

The operative words in the above quote are *make it*. Take the best ideas from brainstorming sessions to a higher degree of resolution and detail by *building a model or prototyping the solution*. A model or prototype is not necessarily an object or building; it is some sort of solution or "deliverable." For example, it could be anything from a strategy, an

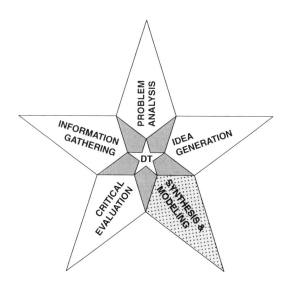

app, story, or experience, to a business model that functions as a demonstration—an "operational prototype"—of the idea.

This phase of design thinking involves narrowing down all the ideas from brainstorming to those that are the most promising (*convergent* thinking). Revisit the problem definition and apply the design criteria set forth therein to help select and focus on the most suitable—and inspiring—ideas. This certainly involves a shift in mindset from idea generation, which, in contrast, could be characterized as *divergent* thinking.

There are two significant goals of creating a model. The first is using the act of creating the model as a tool to develop an idea into a coherent solution. Making things—whether it be a physical three-dimensional model or a narrative description of a strategy—is crucial to innovation (and in many circumstances, funding). "You can think about how you might do something, but cogitating will only get you so far. Sometimes it takes building a prototype to have that Eureka moment,"[23] says Martin Culpepper, a professor of mechanical engineering at MIT. For example, build a crude study model out of cardboard: rip it apart, change something, rebuild it. *Experiment. Play. Explore.* There are similar analogies in working with other media such as writing, drawing, or digital. You can cut and paste words and sentences as easily as you can cut and paste a piece of cardboard.

Do not underestimate the power of serendipity when building a prototype. Creative work is frequently manifest by varying, shifting, and merging elements of the model, whether they are words, sentences, parts of an outline, pieces of cardboard, tracing paper overlays of thick marker diagrams, spreadsheets, photos, or digital layers. Be curious—see where the modeling takes you. Whatever tool you use to construct the model—drawing, writing, model building—should help you to think conceptually. This is an exciting part of design thinking because you don't really know the outcome, and there are so many great possibilities.

see Chapter 3, Tools and strategies.

The prototype should facilitate a "conversation" between the design thinker and the project. Build quickly and keep the dialogue flowing. "Ambiguity and abstraction are particularly important at the early stages of conceptualization because they provide the opportunity for the recall and creative association of ideas from memory."[24] Moreover, do not take time to strive for perfection; the first few iterations are "drafts," that is, they will likely be developed and improved upon.

The second objective in building a model is to get feedback through testing and critical evaluation. The model, therefore, should be a very close embodiment of a proposed (draft) solution in order to elicit the most constructive comments and critique. (See the next section, Critical evaluation, below.)

Always keep the following axioms in mind during the "synthesis through modeling" phase:

- Consider stakeholders' perspectives at every step of prototype development.

- Pursue several alternatives concurrently for critical evaluation by others.

- Responses to early prototypes may provide new information and insights that could alter the direction of subsequent prototype development.

- No matter how brilliant an idea appears on paper, a (functioning) prototype is what becomes a persuasive alternative.

CRITICAL EVALUATION

Having frequent conversations about the work—exposing it to criticism—with people of *diverse backgrounds and experiences* can serve to amplify or refine ideas, eliminate ideas, or suggest new ideas. I would underscore the importance of seeking challenges from individuals with varied perspectives and skill sets (particularly those whose points of view are not aligned with yours)—harnessing and synthesizing their ideas in synergistic fashion can help us all do better in whatever tasks we undertake. Indeed, valid criticism should be considered an opportunity to learn, and improve the work. Dialogues

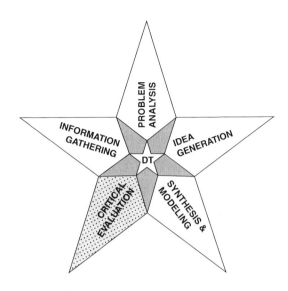

and criticism are therefore among the most essential tools to arrive at the best possible solutions.

See Chapter 5 Business > Creativity in the culinary arts.

Why is feedback so important? Madlen Simon elaborates:

> Conversations and critiques help design thinkers to personally reflect on the process. When you have to articulate an idea and respond to criticism you are forced to think through more aspects of an issue, and ideas tend to become more concrete. On the other hand, if you keep something locked inside your head without having a dialogue, the reflection phase is neglected as you charge forward, with potential loss of opportunities and insights.[25]

> Change or adjustment in response to criticism does not have to be seen as compromise, but as something that makes a project more sensitive and responsive to some special issue.

Critical feedback can also help to shed light on the various viewpoints of complicated issues thereby ensuring that all aspects of a problem are considered.

Note an important caveat. All this is not to say that you should always be unconditionally deferential and subservient to criticism. There are times when comments may be frankly absurd, off the mark, or just plain wrong, and you have to recognize that someone else may have an agenda that might not be in your project's best interests. So attend carefully to critical challenges, extract the best of it, and build on it, but readily acknowledge and dismiss what is clearly off base or irrelevant.

External criticism

This last component of the iterative loop is so influential in shaping the final outcome. Embrace pragmatic and appropriate feedback on models or prototypes, be it from stakeholders, peers, experts or specialists, and anyone else who might be even tangentially relevant to the work. Integrating feedback in real time—as it becomes available—into the loop is a unique attribute of design thinking.

Change or adjustment in response to criticism does not have to be seen as compromise, but as something that makes a project more sensitive and responsive to some special issue that may not have been illuminated if not for the additional attention. Another response to criticism is to think of the project as a completely different assignment, which demonstrates that there are many ways to approach a problem. I actually look forward to constructive criticism because the work usually gets better.

An added benefit of responding to constructive suggestions from stakeholders, especially if it represents a genuine and substantive contribution, is that the stakeholder will be that much more invested in the project. Be sure to reference an idea the stakeholder proposed, squiggled on the back of a napkin, or shown as a precedent from another similar problem. Point out how, for example, the squiggle triggered an idea, was translated into some aspect of the solution, or was influential in making a design decision.

See Chapter 4 Politics and society > Expanding the politics of civic engagement > Writing and passing the Congressional Accountability Act.

It is not always easy to accept and respond to criticism, but there are several truisms that are important to keep in mind in order to derive the most from feedback. The most obvious and important one is to avoid the natural propensity for being defensive. Try to understand precisely what the critic is asserting. If there is any ambiguity, form a hypothesis about what is being said and try to restate the critic's comments. In this way, clarification is more likely (the critic may elaborate in valuable fashion), and you demonstrate your efforts at understanding. But more dialogue—and to reiterate this valuable point—can spark a new idea or initiate a line of inquiry not previously imagined that could benefit the work. The cliché that tensions can lead to creativity, or conflicting views tend to stimulate more and deeper thinking, is certainly true as long as participating individuals are healthy and secure enough to be receptive to competing or dissenting ideas.

The art of self-criticism

Cultivate the habit of self-criticism, which can be a powerful component of design thinking. Self-criticism can efficiently inspire new ideas, infuse projects or solutions with special meaning, and help formulate cogent arguments in support of convictions and aspirations. Used properly as a design tool, says Christopher Mead, former dean and professor of Art History and Architecture at the University of New Mexico, self-criticism can serve to test the strength of initial ideas against the problem definition, mission, or mandate. Once the value of those ideas has been proven, continue to test to ensure their coherent development by editing out missteps or flaws.[26] When critically reflecting about a solution, ensure that every decision, move, or idea relates to the bigger concept in some way.

> See Chapter 8 Writing > Draft as prototype.

Be your own devil's advocate. Pose tough questions about potential solutions and their consequences.[27] This simulation of creative tension can be a catalyst for thinking about other very different groundbreaking alternatives as well as an effective strategy to help recognize shortcomings.

Christopher Mead succinctly summarizes the value of criticism in relation to design thinking: "Criticism can make us see familiar things from new perspectives, shake us out of our shopworn habits, and provoke us into thinking about problems we might otherwise overlook."[28] I would add that critical evaluation helps to make solutions optimally responsive to stakeholders and context, cost effective, and artful. Seek as much feedback as possible; it will enrich your work.

NOTES

1   Clifford Geertz, *The Interpretation of Cultures*, New York: Basic Books, 1973, pp. 5–6, 9–10.

2   Alice Waugh, "Constraints and Viewpoints," *Spectrum*, Massachusetts Institute of Technology, Winter 2017, p. 11.

3   Madlen Simon, interview by the author, College Park, MD, May 6, 2016.

4   Ibid.

5   Steve Martin, *Born Standing Up: A Comic's Life*, New York: Scribner, 2007, p. 192.

6   Ibid.

7   Ibid.

8   Mark Robert Johnson, FAIA, interview by the author, Washington, DC, July 21, 2016.

9   Ralph Waldo Emerson, "Address Before the Senior Class," at Harvard Divinity School, 1838 (see www.harvardsquarelibrary.org/biographies/emersons-divinity-school-address [accessed on September 5, 2017]).

10 Peter G. Rowe, *Design Thinking*, Cambridge, MA: The MIT Press, 1987.

11 Ashley Browning, Christine Ortiz, and Mary C. Boyce, "Mechanics of Composite Elasmoid Fish Scale Assemblies and Their Bioinspired Analogues," *Journal of the Mechanical Behavior of Biomedical Materials*, vol. 19, March 2013, pp. 75–86.

12 Paul J. H. Schoemaker and Steven Krupp, "The Power of Asking Pivotal Questions," *MIT Sloan Management Review*, December 14, 2014 (see sloanreview.mit.edu/article/the-power-of-asking pivotal-questions).

13 Steven Spielberg, speaking at Harvard's commencement, May 26, 2016.

14 See Andrew Pressman, *Designing Relationships: The Art of Collaboration in Architecture*, Abingdon: Routledge, 2014.

15 Alex F. Osborn, *Applied Imagination: Principles and Procedures of Creative Thinking*, New York: Scribner 1979 (first printing 1953), pp. 297–301.

16 Mark Robert Johnson, FAIA, interview by the author, Washington, DC, July 21, 2016.

17 Clark Kellogg, "Focus on the Future: Learning from Studio," *Design Intelligence Knowledge Reports*, January 2006, p. 9.

18 Jeannette M. Wing, "Computational Thinking," *Communications of the ACM*, vol. 49, no. 3, March 2006, p. 33.

19 Tom Kelley and Jonathan Littman, *The Art of Innovation: Lessons in Creativity from IDEO, America's Leading Design Firm*, New York: Currency/Doubleday, 2001, p. 232.

20 Christine Hauser and Christina Anderson, "At this Museum, Failures are Welcome," *The New York Times*, April 25, 2017, www.nytimes.com/2017/04/25/arts/museum-of-failure.html [accessed on April 21, 2017].

21 Don Metz, *Confessions of a Country Architect*, Piermont, NH: Bunker Hill Publishing, 2007, p. 101.

22 Excluding Europe: THEME FROM "NEW YORK, NEW YORK"

23 Quoted from Elizabeth Thomson, "In Praise of Building: MIT's Maker Czar Celebrates Hands-On Learning," *MIT Spectrum*, Spring 2015, p. 10.

24 Richard Nordhaus, "Drawing on the Computer," in Andrew Pressman, *Professional Practice 101*, New York: Wiley, 1997, p. 258.

25 Madlen Simon, interview by the author, College Park, MD, May 6, 2016.

26 Christopher Mead, paraphrased by Andrew Pressman in "It's Not Personal, It's Business: Peer Review and Self-Criticism Are Crucial Tools that Elevate the Quality of Preliminary Designs," *Architectural Record*, vol. 187, no. 9, September 1999, p. 28.

27 For more information and related research see Paul J. H. Schoemaker and Steven Krupp, "The Power of Asking Pivotal Questions," *MIT Sloan Management Review*, December 14, 2014 (see sloanreview.mit.edu/article/the-power-of-asking pivotal-questions).

28 Christopher Mead, "Critical Thinking in Architectural Design," in *Architectural Design Portable Handbook*, New York: McGraw-Hill, 2001, pp. 42–44.

3

TOOLS AND STRATEGIES

This chapter of *Design Thinking* describes various tools and strategies that can nurture curiosity, exploration and discovery, advance the design-thinking process, and promote means to arrive at optimal solutions. Explicitly outlining a problem and delineating proposed solutions in some readily

New ideas may become apparent as a function of simply *utilizing* the appropriate tool.

accessible medium such as drawing and diagramming, working with spreadsheets, a whiteboard, even photographing, can be a great strategy to effectively think about it. New ideas may become apparent as a function of simply *utilizing* the appropriate tool.

DIAGRAMMING

Converting information into forms that are analytically illuminating can be quite useful. It can also inspire creativity. Visual depiction of data invariably helps design thinkers—and stakeholders—to understand problems more precisely and to think about possibilities for their solutions. Rough sketches can facilitate efficient organization of material; to underscore (or suggest) hierarchy and relationships between elements of a problem, and make it easy to discern patterns. Grouping similar elements—or recombining the elements in new ways—can likewise be revealing. The ultimate goal of diagramming is to explore—think through the problem—and then to "capture an idea,"[1] and, finally, to communicate the idea.

See Chapter 5 Business > Visioning, listening, and diagramming at a university > Diagramming.

I would broadly define diagramming as including bubble diagrams, mind maps, flow charts, organizational structures, decision trees, concept maps, outlines or bulleted lists, and even blocks of text on Post-its (see Figures 3.1 and 3.2)—anything that visually depicts information. Post-its are especially easy to move and therefore are

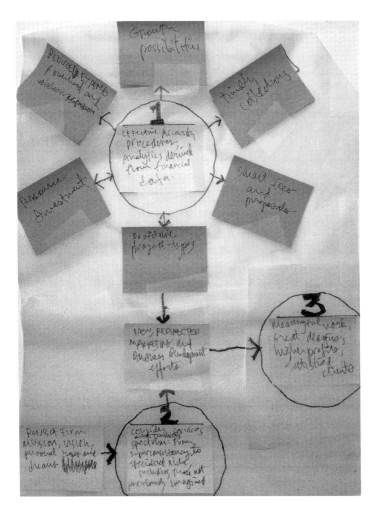

Figure 3.1 Evolution of a diagram: 1 of 2. The ubiquitous Post-its are ubiquitous for a reason: they are easy to use and manipulate. Here, thoughts are posted with a first attempt at organizing them.

Source: The author.

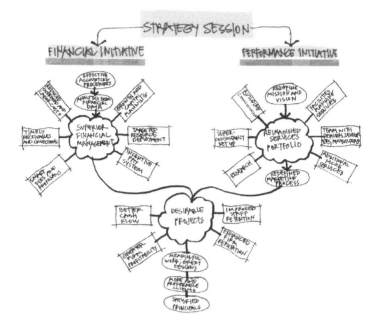

Figure 3.2 Evolution of a diagram: 2 of 2. Converting Post-its and building on them to arrive at a final diagram.

Source: The author.

easy to play with and experiment (the ubiquitous Post-it Notes are a staple for good reason).

The bubbles in bubble diagrams are abstract graphic representations of some element, and are easy to manipulate. Lines connecting bubbles can be quite meaningful in suggesting the relationship between those bubbles. For example, a solid heavy line with arrows on one or both ends could be a direct relationship; a dotted or light line can imply a secondary relationship, and so on. Varying shapes (i.e., circles, squares) and colors can highlight or differentiate elements and categories. One key to making effective diagrams is to annotate the bubbles or boxes profusely as a way to convey additional information that doesn't lend itself to a graphic, and that fully elaborates the content.

Everyone has the capability to draw quick and unrefined diagrams — just think about the proverbial napkin sketch. Some of the most creative work is done on the back of a napkin on an airplane. Without any expectations, doodling, as a precursor to diagramming, is one strategy that can jumpstart more meaningful sketching, and might even lead to a serendipitous breakthrough.

Everyone has a favorite pen or marker. A soft pencil, thick marker, or fountain pen on plain white bond paper, newsprint, brown butcher paper, yellow trace, or a whiteboard holds a raw sensual appeal. There is an inherent pleasure—a mélange of tactile, visual, and auditory stimuli that invite you to continue drawing. Take full advantage of this great medium in thinking about the issues.

On the other hand, for those who are more comfortable in the digital realm, there are numerous apps for sketching, doodling, and creating diagrams. While drawings from these apps look great, I would caution that the end result should not be about how the diagram looks or how it is constructed, but that it is a helpful tool for exploration of ideas. "Technology is powerful, but sometimes it can make you less flexible, especially in the early stages of design,"[2] says Maria Yang, founder and director of MIT's Ideation Lab.

I would add that sketching is such a great tool because it is the most immediate brain-to-hand means of expression. It truly enhances creative thinking. In the immortal words of Donald Schön, drawing enables a "reflective conversation with the situation [you] are shaping."[3] Moreover, there is an ambiguity to the lines in rough freehand sketches, which is appropriate for conceptual thinking.

Framing the problem in visual terms is a basic strategy from the design thinking toolbox, and presents a different way of examining ideas for possible solutions. Going through the exercise of laying out the components of a problem—visually depicting and ordering them—can facilitate a necessary familiarity with pragmatic issues, and suggest possible relationships and connections, an emerging recipe, that heretofore was not considered or even imagined.

REFLECTING

Perhaps one of the most overlooked yet readily available tools for modeling and promoting design thinking is *a dog*—especially for people who have a home office. This is an excellent suggestion from Michael Tardif.[4] A dog will ensure essential time for reflection, which will perhaps set the stage for that Eureka moment. While working on a problem, after examining all the pertinent information and prior to making any substantive or key decisions, put it aside to let it incubate. Insist on a creative pause after an intensive work session, and take the dog for a walk. Talk to your dog, meet its curious and wide-eyed, head-tilted gaze. Consider alternate ideas and approaches. Present them to your unconditionally loyal and furry friend.

View the dog walk as an opportunity for the creative pause—to unwind and relax (see Figure 3.3). And be sure to leave your smartphone at home so there are no interruptions. "When stuck . . . step away, get some distance and then try again. Sleep on data since the mind continues to process information when resting."[5] Let the ideas percolate. Even if you don't have a dog, budget time for reflecting on all the information gathered to date; on failed attempts to solve the problem; and on the larger questions to see new perspectives.

If frozen and the work is not advancing, come back to the problem at a later time from a different viewpoint. Reflecting may put you in the right mindset. Isolate the issue; do more research, become more

Figure 3.3 A dog will ensure essential time for reflection—a creative pause to unwind and relax—to perhaps set the stage for that Eureka moment.

Source: The author.

informed about it. Change the medium in which you are working (i.e., hand drawing, an app, writing, whiteboard, etc.). Alter your routine: work later or start earlier. Vary your environment: go to a good coffee shop or library. Insights may strike you while taking a shower. Focus on a small idea rather than trying to find the big idea.

Do not underestimate the value of downtime, of dogtime. Ideas take time to grow. Sometimes working on an unrelated task and not thinking about the problem will yield insights later on. Acknowledge

Time for reflection is crucial for making sense of all the information, and for discovering meaningful insights.

that not everything has to be considered billable time. Time for reflection is crucial for making sense of all the information, and for discovering meaningful insights. Time for man's best friend is crucial for a positive outlook on life as well as the problem at hand.

PRESENTING

Presenting prototypes, solutions, or alternative schemes to stakeholders is a key step in the design-thinking process. Great work ends up on the cutting-room floor if stakeholders do not perceive that it is great. It therefore behooves the design thinker to engage stakeholders in a discussion that includes the following: (1) A thorough understanding of the problem and surrounding issues; (2) a description of those who are impacted by the problem and its potential solution; and (3) an explanation of the solution and how it brilliantly addresses the problem.

Presumably, if the stakeholders have been part of the process at every step, then there should be little mystery about how the solution was developed. If not, reveal some of the process of working through the problem since inception, and explain how ideas evolved and informed the final solution. Justify major design decisions—clarify how they are accountable in some way (i.e., not arbitrary). Show initial prototypes that were used to test ideas and advance the work, which may also demonstrate how stakeholders' input was incorporated into the work.

According to Weld Coxe, who was a founding principal of one of the premier consultancies in management of professional service firms, *the objective of an effective presentation is to project a fresh idea and have it acted upon.* Salesmanship comes into play; "The techniques used," says Coxe, "will vary considerably according to the nature of the idea and the audience to be reached."[6] The logical conclusion to Weld's statement is to think about the presentation as a design problem. How would you tailor the presentation of your solution, and to whom, so that it would be optimally received?

Another useful perspective is to view the application of negotiating skills as a tool for productive conversations about the work. Excellent negotiating skills can be relevant to educating and selling stake-holders on design possibilities. Particularly noteworthy is the idea of "principled negotiation," proposed by Roger Fisher and William Ury in their classic book on negotiation *Getting to Yes*, in which they recommend that issues be decided on their merits. An important caveat is to recognize that everyone theoretically ought to be on the same team, sharing the same goals. The "negotiation" should then be viewed as a mechanism for mutual understanding and enlightenment toward creating a better solution, not as something to win.[7]

Notes on verbal presentations

Below are some essential strategies for engaging in a constructive dialogue and effectively communicating with stakeholders.

- **Project confidence**. This is obviously easy to do when you know what you're talking about. Moreover, be passionate about the work, and be sure to express genuine, authentic enthusiasm. Convert any initial nervousness into excitement. Be animated and energetic. And enjoy the experience.

- **"Grab" the audience**. The overarching idea for the solution should be a natural hook. Be persuasive—build the entire presentation around this central focus, and support the hook with other relevant points. Being persuasive often simply amounts to illuminating a well-studied idea. Engaging the audience is just as important as grabbing the audience's attention: a conversation can be a great way to be inclusive and promote the work.

- **Speak clearly and without jargon**. Try not to patronize people by an exaggerated or simplified lecture; encourage questions and respond with a level of detail commensurate with the inquiry.

- **Ensure that the presentation is succinct**. Be aware that some people may have the attention span of a gnat. There will always be time to elaborate if there are follow-up questions. Take time to crystallize thoughts—*prepare* for the presentation.

- **Be mindful of the basics**. While speaking, vary cadence and volume to help keep everyone interested; avoid droning on and on in a monotone. It almost goes without saying how important it is to maintain eye contact with the audience. And move around—don't be shy about striding away from a desk or lectern—try to get up-close and personal.

Notes on graphic presentations

Always think about how a scheme will be framed—both graphically and verbally—in ways that will be understandable and exciting to the stakeholders. Realize that a good solution can look bad by not paying enough attention to professional quality in its presentation.

- **First, do no harm**. With all the stunning graphic technology, templates, animation, and slick slideshow programs at our disposal, it is easy for the format to overshadow the content. So the basic rule is: never draw attention to the presentation mode; whatever medium is selected should support content not distract from it.

- **Annotate drawings or diagrams**. Explanations complement the graphics and facilitate greater understanding. This point was mentioned earlier in this chapter but it is so important, and frequently ignored, that it is worth underscoring.

- **Create a focus**. Just as the verbal presentation should have a hook, so too should each graphic element have a central focus. It makes it easier and more interesting to read, and indicates what is most important. The graphic focus could be larger, bolder, more colorful, or rendered with more detail than its surroundings. Try to avoid using exclusively equally-weighted elements on a slide or graphic. This is the graphic analogy to avoid droning on in a monotone.

- **Be judicious with special graphic treatment**. For example, *a little bit* of color can have a big impact when applied in the right place at the right time. Color is terrific, but only if it enhances the message—its essence and uniqueness. Its use shouldn't be arbitrary. You don't necessarily need to use a whole spectrum of colors—one or two might be most effective for any given presentation.

- **Prepare a summary package**. There's nothing like a compelling take-away of text and/or graphics to help sell a solution.

NOTES

1 Scott Berinato, "Visualizations That Really Work," *Harvard Business Review*, June 2016, pp. 94–100.

2 Ken Shulman, "Maria Yang: The Prototype Moment," *Spectrum*, Massachusetts Institute of Technology, Winter 2017, pp. 19–20.

3 Donald A. Schön, *The Reflective Practitioner: How Professionals Think in Action*, New York: Basic Books, 1983, p. 103.

4 Michael Tardif, Personal communication with the author, May 5, 2016.

5 Paul J. H. Schoemaker and Steven Krupp, "The Power of Asking Pivotal Questions," *MIT Sloan Management Review*, December 14, 2014, p. 9 (see sloanreview.mit.edu/article/the-power-of-askingpivotal-questions).

6 Weld Coxe, *Marketing Architectural and Engineering Services*, Second Edition, New York: Van Nostrand Reinhold, 1983.

7 Roger Fisher and William Ury, *Getting to Yes: Negotiating Agreement Without Giving In*, Second Edition, New York: Penguin Books, 1991.

Part 2

APPLICATIONS

Have other professions, industries, or fields adopted—or adapted—design thinking? Does design thinking represent an innovative creative approach to solving problems, developing fresh projects and services, and reconciling conflicts? Why does design thinking appear to be attracting so much attention across disciplines in both academic and professional settings? Part 2 will address these questions by example, and demonstrate that design thinking is certainly not limited to architects and the traditional design fields.

This section incorporates new research and information from a variety of sources ranging from professionals who routinely use design thinking as a component of their jobs to academics who teach courses in design thinking. A series of vignettes derived from real-life examples—with which many readers will readily identify—will highlight how design thinking can help to solve problems or do work that is particularly challenging and fraught with constraints, and that requires creativity and innovation. Many of the stories are drawn directly from my interviews, while others are culled from secondary sources.

It will be quite apparent that those with different sets of disciplinary knowledge can take advantage of design thinking methodology to solve problems creatively—and optimally. In the spirit of the cliché that a method is only as good as its application, the following snippets reveal successful applications of design thinking in such diverse areas as politics, diplomacy, leadership, business, health, law, and writing. It is hoped that some of the lessons from these applications are generalizable to readers' unique situations, and will inspire more widespread use of design thinking.

4

POLITICS AND SOCIETY

Design thinking can be a critical tool for addressing leadership challenges. Design thinking promotes visualization of the big picture, reframing of perspectives, creation of innovative solutions to problems, attention to detail, and management and reconciliation of diverse and complex interests and relationships. Cultivating an attitude to authentically listen to insights from others as well successfully sharing one's own vision may not always be easy but can be very effective as illustrated in the following vignettes.

EXPANDING THE POLITICS OF CIVIC ENGAGEMENT

A good leader uses the design process as a model that allows everyone to participate and thus improves and expands the politics of civic engagement.[1]

The most creative and productive way [to apply design thinking] is to engage people—the [stakeholders]—in the process.[2]

Richard Swett

Richard N. Swett was elected to the US Congress and served as the US Ambassador to Denmark.

Dick underscores a fundamental aspect of design thinking that leads to successful resolution of problems or great projects that are rich in meaning: *be inclusive*. The magic occurs when the input is creatively interpreted, and stakeholders see or are explicitly shown how their ideas influenced the outcome. The stakeholders are then more likely to be fully invested in that outcome, which is so important for success. This creative interpretation may reveal windows of opportunity not previously contemplated, and may thereby provide extraordinary solutions that are also responsive to stakeholder requirements and preferences.

A leader who applies design thinking is someone who has a vision, understands where he or she is going to direct the process, but is not confined by the boundaries or preconceptions of what a solution could be. The design thinking method will allow—even encourage—everyone who is participating in formulating the solution to make their contributions, and the solution will then emerge. It could be a political, business, or some other organizational context where there is a need for leadership, but also where there is the likely benefit of participation. The end result is not clearly defined; rather, engagement with the whole process takes the team to a solution. (See Chapter 5, "Implementing a strategic technology plan" for a very different perspective, one in which the desired outcome is known but the pieces leading to that outcome are the variables.)

A caveat worth noting is that this type of leadership requires some assertiveness and presence; a design-by-committee environment can be frightening if the leader does not have the confidence to control the dialogue in that environment.

Dick recommends working toward the best solution for *all* the stakeholders, perhaps promoting a shared vision of project objectives from the outset. If design thinking is utilized in its truest, purist sense, the end result can sometimes be a surprise. But as long as it is a better surprise than what everybody had in mind, then that's okay.

Writing and passing the Congressional Accountability Act

Dick co-authored the Congressional Accountability Act, landmark legislation that requires Congress to abide by the same laws it passes for the rest of the country. I asked Dick how he was able to harness inclusive participation in order to get this landmark legislation passed.

The typical process in Congress involved first writing a bill, then seeking cosponsors, and finally the bill goes to the floor of the House of Representatives where people try to pin amendments to it in order to change what they don't like. Dick suggested,

> Why don't we do this like we're designing a building: let's go around with a blank piece of paper to all the different groups that are interested in the accountability, and let's ask them to tell us how to design this, and we will interpret, integrate, and synthesize their different designs. We will come up with an amalgam of the best of what they have told us.[3]

Members are not all going to do this in the same room at the same time. The idea was so totally foreign to them that no one really understood what was going on—so much so that Norm Ornstein at one point said,

> Wait a minute, you guys are letting everybody say what they think your legislation should be, and then you're going to come back to them with three different schemes to review, then they'll pick the one that they like the best?![4]

Dick responded, "That's exactly what we're going to do." Ornstein said that this is fascinating because no one has ever taken this approach in this body before.

It took three and a half years to complete the legislation; Dick and his coauthors had to threaten everybody because they weren't moving the bill to the floor for a vote. Congressional members didn't want to be made accountable because they had this great House rules system where they could do whatever they pleased—their behavior never had to be connected to the laws that were passed for the rest of the country. Dick and others finally forced the vote; they won 97–3 in the Senate and something like 433–3 in the House. It passed by an overwhelming margin because everyone was participating and yet Dick and his coauthors were still able to give this direction and to maintain a sense of control over what they were ultimately trying to achieve. It was a captivating exercise.

Part of the creativity lies in how Dick was able to *interpret the input in a way that was meaningful and effective* while everyone felt as though they were invested in its content (Figure 4.1).

Figure 4.1 It is important for stakeholders to appreciate how they have influenced the "design" solution. For example, point out something like: "This squiggle in the final design is the direct result of your comment on our initial draft."

Source: The author.

Overhauling the management structure at the US embassy, Denmark

In Copenhagen, morale at the embassy was "in the pits." When Dick first arrived as the Ambassador, he couldn't understand why people were unhappy, after all, this was Denmark—a wonderful place. There were 16 different agencies at the embassy at that time; all separate silos, and no one talked across those silos. There was a community of 250 Americans and foreign service nationals, all presumably working together, and yet there was little connection between them that would enable them to understand what their colleagues were doing, or to even identify their colleagues.

It was clear that this situation called for some kind of team-based management system. Dick wanted to create teams of people who would work together and use their creative connections to not only get to know each other but also to come up with more imaginative and hopefully less expensive solutions to the myriad of problems they were facing.

It took a year to realize that no one wanted to embrace the team-based structure. Dick tried to promote the idea and taught critical path management among other project management skills and tools. But he finally figured out that the staff was stymied by the term "team." Team was anathema in this bureaucracy, meaning nobody gets credit and therefore nobody advances. Dick then understood how to approach this issue.

Dick declared that each team would be made up of 6–8 people, with only one from each agency. There would be agencies represented on every team, each of which was formed around projects such as issue campaigns and diplomatic dialogues. The embassy teams would be similar to the teams that form around projects in an architecture firm. Instead of using building materials, they used information as their building blocks. Instead of designing office structures, they designed information structures for scheduling and measuring results on complicated interrelated diplomatic discussions.

The typical staff response was, "Why did you stick all these people on this team who know nothing about what I am doing?" Dick replied,

> First, you sell them and yourself short because you'll serve on another team in the same capacity that they're serving on your team. That is, you're going to be an objective observer who is going to look at everything that is being done by that team— not through the eyes of the specialist, who thinks they know everything there is to know about that particular subject, but through the eyes of an observer from a distance who might see that there's a way to do something a little differently and a little bit better because they have a different perspective on the world. That doesn't take from your authority to give direction and vision to this team but you better listen to what these people have to say because their suggestions will make your decisions better.[5]

Implementing this new approach took time and training. Morale went way up. Everybody was enjoying work because they were being challenged, and they were discovering that they were able to find genuinely interesting solutions that were better than what they had previously.

It is important to empower teams by giving them the opportunity to authentically give voice to their desires. Architects are aware that their clients' level of sophistication varies. The less educated a client is about design, the more time is spent educating them to help them understand, for example, why spatial relationships are planned in a certain way. This analogy applies to most team situations. It is necessary to first understand the basic level of competency of the team so the baseline from which they can start making choices can be established. The team should be given the opportunity to make decisions and then see those decisions actually being accepted and implemented into the program; This yields ownership or what amounts to "sweat equity" with respect to the program.

Many managers are frightened because they don't understand how to empower a team and yet remain at the helm; this is very much a learned skill that is shaped by design thinking.

The presence of clients and stakeholders is what distinguishes architecture from art and makes it one of the great professions. Artists make great sculptures, but ostensibly the work may only be about the artist. An architect, on the other hand, is one who creates a great building design that responds to the needs of the client *and* that has a special aesthetic about it that expresses what it does for the client and the community.

Dick's observations demonstrate that to arrive at the best solution, design thinking does not have to be limited to a unilateral vision of a single individual; it requires skill to compromise in some ideal sense (or redesign to make the work better); and develops a meaningful interactive relationship with stakeholders.

MANAGING GRIDLOCKED DEBATES

> In doing my job every day on behalf of Carmel, I have seen first-hand that design thinking can be transformative to gridlocked debates.[6]

> Victoria Beach

Victoria Beach is a member of the Carmel City Council, California, where she has served for the last four years, including a one-year stint as Vice Mayor. In the following two stories she demonstrates how design thinking can be transformative in the management of grid-locked debates, and how it has helped her to resolve some wicked problems in the political arena.

An all too common reality in politics is an "us versus them" scenario in which stakeholders are entrenched in one position or another. One of Victoria's insights is that dealing with such a conflict should *not* be about persuading others to your point of view, which is frequently an exercise in futility. Rather, the strategy should be to apply design thinking to create or identify and then focus on a different path, not previously imagined. In this way, *conflicts can become opportunities for progress*.

This approach requires a certain calm maturity, a realization that an initial position is not necessarily precious, and that there are multiple solutions to a problem. Nothing is that special or brilliant that it can't be built upon or changed for the good of a project or support of an issue. Unlike mathematics where there is one right answer, in politics (as in architectural design) there may be a multiplicity of alternatives that can work. Design thinking can help to formulate an optimal one. So, table the argument for a moment and frame the problem in a different way.

Given the volatility of the current political climate, according to Victoria, "design thinking is not a luxury for society—it's a necessity."

Flanders Mansion: creating an option not previously imagined

Carmel, California, is a small picturesque village with a stunning beach and a bluff shaded by cyprus trees. Behind the rows of quaint shops there is a grid of small cottages, which are all sited within a forest of green. It is a visionary place, developed a hundred years ago as an artists' community and a home for academics.

Flanders Mansion, a vacant historic home within Carmel's largest park, had been at the heart of an impassioned controversy about its use for many years. It has been the focus of multiple lawsuits involving millions of dollars, environmental impact reviews, and even a referendum.

The issue: sell the mansion and make some money for the city (advocated by the City Council) or preserve it for public functions. But it's more complicated than that. Unfortunately, since the mansion is not located at the edge of the park, it can't be carved out as a discrete piece. If it were to be sold, a path to the building (complete with a fence to keep the public out) would be required for owners' access—but this would clearly disrupt the flow of the park. Many residents fought vigorously against this idea, dividing the peaceful little town; there was acrimony and vitriol, it was just awful.

Even though there was a referendum and a clear winner (approving the proposed sale), a strong minority was still protesting, "You just can't do that to the park." The City Council's position was that if the courts require divestment because of the vote, no one on the council was going to break the law.

An arduous state environmental impact review is required in California so that a municipality cannot carelessly divest itself of public parkland. In this case, wildlife migration routes were potentially at risk. If a sale were to take place, the new owners would be responsible for "scientific" compliance on an annual basis to protect native animals.

The referendum had *not* been based on projections about how much the city coffers would benefit from a sale. Realtors typically use a comparable to establish an asking price. There is no "comp" for a place like Flanders that accounted for its lizard and bat requirements, fencing and access issues, and the ongoing public dispute.

Essentially, an owner would have to play the role of a park ranger or eco-biologist while living there, costing hundreds of dollars per year, not to mention the possibility of hostile residents protesting every time the owner used the driveway. In other words, this was not necessarily a slam-dunk for a multi-million dollar sale.

At this point, Victoria examined the city's budget, which had a line item for care of parkland. The Flanders Mansion was a fraction below one percent of the total budget. So this was not some albatross around the neck of the city.

Also noteworthy is that this structure was placed on the historic register. This fact removed any option of demolition. Maintenance costs are not salient since the unusual structure is made entirely of concrete. Not much has to be done to maintain it except for con-ducting periodic checks to ensure, for example, that the windows are not cracked and the bats are squeaking happily.

In summary, Faction A said, "You can't destroy or diminish the public park; there would be a major scar if a big piece were cut out of it. Selling it would interrupt the flow and enjoyment of the park." Faction B insisted, "We need money for our coffers; and we certainly can't have waste in the budget with the Mansion draining it every year. Who can argue with fiscal health?" This was intractable.

At a council meeting Victoria reviewed newly uncovered facts as a result of her research and consultations with experts, including maintenance people who had worked on the Mansion and prior park administrators. These facts, which had not been discussed before, included the relatively good health of the building, the lack of expense in maintaining it, and the comp issue and environ-mental requirements for a new owner in the event of a sale.

After ten minutes of presenting these facts, Victoria proposed a new solution: put the Flanders Mansion on the back burner and

The mature designer is always ready to try something else, is not afraid of information, and is not afraid that he or she would not have another idea.

think of it as a folly in the park. In other words, essentially *do nothing and stop talking about it* (simply talking about it costs the town a lot of money that could otherwise be spent more constructively). This option was never imagined because everyone was so entrenched in his or her own position.

In the political arena, people typically take sides on issues—similar to partisanship—that *must* be adhered to. But that's just a construct; sometimes the best solutions have no sides, no conflicts. Flanders Mansion is an example of an *individual* applying design thinking to find a different research-based solution to a problem that had pitted neighbors against neighbors for decades with millions of dollars wasted because no one was looking for a non-conflict solution.

Victoria paraphrases one of her teachers in her analysis of this story.

> The mature designer is always ready to try something else, is not afraid of information, and is not afraid that he or she would not have another idea. Fear of not producing is common: the blank page; what am I going to say; maybe I can't solve this. If you are going in a direction that's not fruitful, or you don't know whether it's working and you have no way to test it, never be afraid to jettison it, critique it, or throw it to the side and try something else and then assess which option is best.[7]

When attempting to resolve a dispute it is essential to be objective; to work at avoiding rigid investment in any one position. I realize this may be redundant, but it is an insight worth repeating. Victoria offers an example from architectural practice:

Figure 4.2 Empathic understanding is fundamental to design thinking. As the Flanders Mansion vignette illustrates, the focus of problem solving should not necessarily be about vigorous advocacy of a position, but rather the motives underlying the position in order to prompt a fresh solution.

Source: The author.

If you have two warring clients, a husband and wife, I always think we're going to find something that they both like if they talk to me in detail and explain the issues. If they help me research what's underlying the conflict, i.e., why don't you want to face south when you're doing the dishes and your spouse must face south, we will get to the placement of the sink that actually makes sense— if I can understand the thinking behind their motives. Analogous to the Mansion, the focus should not be what are we fighting about, rather, what are the underlying motives or structure underneath the positions? That will trigger some other way of thinking.[8]

Focus on procedure to yield desired outcome

In this vignette Victoria demonstrates how to get an initiative (a $20 million trail project) passed in a transportation board meeting by being creative about *procedural issues* rather than advocating for the initiative itself, which would very likely have been an unsuccessful tactic.

The transportation budget for the municipality had to be finalized during a meeting this day in order to promulgate a sales tax increase to fund various projects. The $20 million trail project was also at stake. The elected officials, including Victoria, who were around the table for this large board meeting, were debating whether or not the trail project should be funded. Some were for it, others were against. There was also debate about one other project, a road improvement. Both of these initiatives, the trail and the road, were in a state of uncertainty.

In a great example of community organizing, members of a dozen groups spoke eloquently in favor of the trail project, covering different issues. It was obvious to Victoria that the groups' presentations had been persuasive for board members who had been on the fence, but not to everyone. The supporters' arguments were brilliantly strategic, for example, "Even if you don't like the project the *public* will like it and that will leverage the passage of your sales tax." It was an effective argument because people who really didn't care or who were opposed to the project came to believe that line of thinking might work.

However, there were board members from the powerful committee that was tasked to develop the budget who, despite the arguments for the trail project, were still clearly trying to defeat it. They made a motion that essentially proposed passing certain elements of the project but suggested tabling the specifics. They further proposed forming a subcommittee to study exactly how to deal with the two controversial projects—the trail and the road improvement.

Even though it was well known that Victoria had championed similar trail projects for years and strongly supported this one in particular, she resisted the temptation to weigh-in and remained silent—until the meeting was almost over. It was then that Victoria seized the moment and responded,

> Let's try to avoid forming yet another subcommittee, which will cause delays and prevent us from getting the proposed sales tax issue out to the voters. I think there's a lot of agreement that we need to move forward with the $20 million project—so here is my friendly amendment: accept the trail project and further negotiate items on this last road improvement project that seem resistant to resolution. There was a lot of effective horse-trading earlier in the meeting on other projects; why don't we invoke that same process—with only the concerned parties—for this last item? And then we can leave the room with a fully adopted budget with only a few outstanding details to be worked out for this last project.[9]

That friendly amendment received a nearly unanimous vote so the $20 million trail project that Victoria supported was approved.

Victoria's action was a tactical maneuver that had nothing to do with whether she was in favor of the trail project or not. It was such a seemingly unrelated move that it was not perceived by the advocacy groups as helpful. Members of those groups were confused and upset at the time because they felt Victoria had abandoned them and was not supporting the cause. In fact, Victoria had no intention of leaving the room until their trail project was funded. Success was achieved in the last five minutes when Victoria proposed that friendly amendment. The project would simply not have advanced otherwise.

The vote for action to get the sales tax passed was the means that ultimately led to the project approval. In this case, design thinking influenced the mindset of the politician to step back and not simply be an impassioned but impotent advocate. Rather, the process helped to find a logical, very different and effective angle to advance in order to achieve the desired outcome.

NOTES

1 Richard N. Swett and Colleen M. Thornton, *Leadership by Design*, Atlanta, GA: Greenway Communications, LLC, 2005, p. 302.

2 Ibid. p. 248.

3 Richard Swett, [phone] interview by the author, March 31, 2016.

4 Ibid.

5 Ibid.

6 William Richards, "AIA Voices: Victoria Beach, The Ethicist," *Architect*, February 19, 2015, p. 37.

7 Victoria Beach, [phone] interview by the author, March 2, 2016.

8 Ibid.

9 Ibid.

5

BUSINESS

Design thinking has been recognized as an important means to innovate in the context of developing new products and technologies. But design thinking can also be applied to other business-related challenges such as devising entrepreneurial practice models, expanding professional services, operations, and even setting fees or pricing plans.

There are many cases revealing the value and power of design thinking in the corporate world that have been widely published but are primarily focused on teams—especially managers collaborating with designers. Indeed, many business-school curricula incorporate elective and required courses (in addition to specialized tracks) on design thinking. The vignettes below, however, show how individuals apply design thinking to a very broad range of business problems at varying scales from a self-employed chef to a university president.

IMPLEMENTING A STRATEGIC TECHNOLOGY PLAN

One of the things I so enjoy about my work is that whatever the particular challenge or business problem is, I always take a design approach to developing a solution. One of the most important aspects of that approach is that it enables me to maintain a focus on the "big picture," or overall vision, even as I'm grappling with the weedy details. When talking to other business owners and entrepreneurs, a common refrain is feeling overwhelmed by all the logistical/management details that have to be attended to, and that can suck the life out of your dream. I certainly have my bad days like everyone else, but having a vision and a high tolerance for ambiguity (which is the same as having a high tolerance for risk) are enormously helpful to me. It puts the tedious details of running a business into a larger context and gives those activities meaning.

Michael Tardif

Michael Tardif has over twenty years of experience applying information technologies to the design, construction, operation, and maintenance of buildings. He currently leads Building Informatics Group based in North Bethesda, Maryland.

Strategic plan as jigsaw puzzle

Michael had been asked to develop a strategic technology plan to implement Building Information Modeling software in a construction company—complete with itemized tasks and schedule milestones—and then "drive" implementation of the plan. After studying business operations for three months, he realized that rolling out a strategic plan—executing a linear sequence of steps—would fail because it would be so highly invasive and disruptive to existing business operations. Instead, Michael proposed a vision (or design concept)—a set of measurable goals for the company to achieve—and then set out to achieve those goals opportunistically, in a non-linear fashion, without working out the specifics of execution in advance.

To accomplish this daunting undertaking, Michael invented a brilliant metaphor: "*strategic plan as a jigsaw puzzle*" (Figure 5.1). Michael sought opportunities on different projects to implement portions of the strategic plan; in other words (invoking the metaphor) putting puzzle pieces into place wherever he could. The process was messy and non-linear. Michael and the staff had to synthesize information as it became available, and make adjustments to the "design solution" while maintaining the vision. But the vision always remained clear, and the "complete picture" of the strategic plan emerged over time. This was fundamentally a design-thinking process.

When the process began, Michael knew conceptually what the end result should look like, but didn't quite know how they would get there. If they had waited to have all the detailed elements in

Figure 5.1 Strategic plan as jigsaw puzzle. Insert pieces as appropriate, in nonlinear fashion, to complete the vision.

Source: The author.

place before starting, they would have never started. And they would have failed, because the details would have been wrong, and would have diverted attention from the overall vision they were trying to achieve.

The puzzle metaphor proved more useful than Michael could have dared to hope for. Conversations about the strategic plan revolved around the question, "What piece of the puzzle is that?" Most importantly, at any point in time, no one cared that the picture was incomplete; staff understood that they were moving toward a complete picture, and understood how they were getting there. Michael could have called the strategic planning a design process instead of a jigsaw puzzle, but that metaphor would have been lost on anyone other than architects.

Reimagining electronic information exchange at construction handover

This subhead describes Michael's new business venture. He began by studying the problem, then designing a solution. Every design problem has constraints. The success of any design solution can be measured by how one creatively deals with those constraints. Design thinking requires a willingness to think about constraints and possible solutions conceptually, then testing how each possible solution addresses or overcomes the constraints. It requires recognizing that there isn't a perfect solution to any design problem, only an optimum solution that balances requirements and mitigates the negative impact of the constraints. By looking at the business problem as a design problem, Michael was able to view the constraints differently than others had, and therefore developed insights that led to a completely different business solution than the conventional ones.

When Michael was working at the construction company noted in his first story above, he observed that they were creating rich data packages—information useful to build the projects. There was no way, however, to convey that information to the building owners in any kind of useful fashion. Part of the problem was that the owners weren't asking for it. To make the effort to structure it properly so it would be useful to them was one constraint of the problem. The other was that they weren't explaining what they needed because the people with whom Michael and staff were interacting were the people who were involved in the construction, not the people who would be operating the building.

Michael needed to talk to these people—the facility managers—to find out what information they needed to help operate their building. What was important to them? For example, data on some assets in the building that facility managers must know: serial number, installation date, commissioning date, and so on. There are other assets for which they have no plan—so when they are replaced, it won't be identical, it will be something comparable. The type of information needed is not all that different from one owner to another, but it does vary in its detail depending on the building type and business type.

At conferences, Michael would keep hearing speakers say that owners should drive innovation. He kept thinking, "How do you expect *owners* to drive innovation—they know nothing about it; they don't have the vocabulary. The technology is not designed for their use. The interface is for design and construction, not for operations and management."

For a long time the Holy Grail was the life-cycle building information model, which was going to move from one party to another throughout the building life-cycle, and would be updated along the way. As Michael was contemplating his new venture and talking to building owners he had one question: What are you doing with the model? The response was uniform and profound: "Never touched it; never really opened it."

Michael then started digging into the available data in the models. Even when designers weren't given explicit instructions or direction from the owner about what they wanted in the model, data was there. Maybe not in the right place or not formatted properly, but it was there. Michael realized that the owner was not communicating to the designer what would be useful to them. In the absence of that information, designers make it up: they have to do something. The mundane labeling of rooms is a good example. If the owner doesn't give direction on how spaces should be named and numbered, designers will use their own system that makes sense to them. If they were given that information from owners, it wouldn't take them any more time, but it could be enormously beneficial for the facility managers.

Witness how the equipment is named in modeling. How can this be leveraged? The Eureka Moment: Michael realized that the model doesn't matter—it's the information—it's about mining data from the model. Michael can structure it and put it in some accessible form that is useful to the owner. When the building opens and the facility manager can't change a light bulb, they can't overcome the perception that they don't know what they are doing. Michael's business is to get all that data into their facility management system by the first day of occupancy.

Eureka Moments and intuitive leaps

Michael frequently has Eureka Moments in the course of solving problems. In the first example above, the Eureka Moment was finding the right metaphor—jigsaw puzzle—that others could understand and rally around. That metaphor broke the log-jam both for Michael and the company and enabled them to move forward successfully. In the second example, the Eureka Moment occurred when Michael realized that the problem with conventional "as-built Building Information Modeling (BIM) deliverables" is that the typical building owner doesn't need (or care about) the BIM deliverable at all; what the owner wants is the information in the BIM (i.e., how to access the information in a useful way for the owner). Michael then realized that the problem he was trying to solve was not a technology problem, but a business process and information delivery problem. After that, elements of the optimum solution very quickly emerged.

Eureka Moments don't just happen. All one can do is create the circumstances (via imagination and awareness) that will enable them to occur. It requires a willful temporary suspension of disbelief and—as Michael Graves once famously said—a high tolerance for ambiguity. Design constraints only exist in the physical world; they don't exist in the mind. So, one or more constraints can be held at bay while others are pondered (i.e., look at one piece of the puzzle). Doing this allows analysis of a problem from multiple angles. Eventually a view of the problem comes into focus that suggests one or more potentially viable solutions. Prospective solutions can be tested against the constraints until the best solution is identified and operationalized.

According to Michael's analysis of design thinking, the most important factors to consider when addressing a full spectrum of problems include the following.

- Recognizing that every problem has a solution; not a perfect solution, but an optimum solution (there are always tradeoffs).

- Recognizing that all of the information needed to solve any problem is not available when you start working on the problem.

- Recognizing that you have to begin developing solutions before you have all the information you need to arrive at an optimum solution.

- Recognizing that your process may lead to one or more dead ends, which may require you to rethink your original assumptions.

CREATIVITY IN THE CULINARY ARTS

> Creating a new dish is an iterative process, while cooking efficiently requires a methodical, hierarchical approach.
>
> Francesco Crocenzi

Francesco Crocenzi is the owner and chef of Frankie's Table in Seattle. He creates and packages custom meals, provides personal chef services, and caters custom dinner parties.

Francesco's story demonstrates how design thinking comes to life in the realm of the culinary arts. He believes that anyone can tap into this creative process and apply it. Francesco initially starts with a big idea or inspiration, for example, flavor: "Find an ingredient that intrigues you, then ask, what would taste good with that? What are the relationships of the elements, and how do they affect each other?"

Francesco suggests invoking powerful analytic skills. How do you prepare the ingredients? What heat do you use on the stove? Flavor, texture, and amount of seasoning—how do these things come together? What elements work well together? How can you make it better? Analyze quickly and figure out what needs to be done.

Much of Francesco's cooking for clients is for weekly eating. Many clients have constraints and strict dietary concerns, which must be respected. For example, a client has a no-salt requirement, which is a huge challenge. Salt is so fundamental in Western cooking; people believe that food must have seasoning to bring out flavor. The task is to make the dish flavorful but without salt. That is certainly an area that requires creativity with herbs and spices.

Consider a typical classic dish and apply design thinking to enhance it by searching for precedents, having a vision, and iterating to bring it to a different level while maintaining some of its original characteristics. Francesco finds inspiration from existing recipes and then transforms them into new dishes. Alternatively, he builds on existing recipes to enhance them. He implores us to have a *vision* for a dish. Analyze it and break it down; what are the possibilities for new ingredients? Evolve the dish by iterating: try it one way, test it, modify it, and then repeat the loop.

Francesco states that the most critical elements in design thinking related to creating a new dish are observation and analysis. "When I go into a kitchen," he says, "I can identify the elements by smelling and tasting. When I look at a recipe, I can *envision* what it will be like."

Analysis is the first wave of thought. Then the thinking advances into a creative idea. How does this evolve? What should be changed? What are the options? That is the schematic or preliminary phase. What is

You must listen to that little touch of feedback—it could be a key to the best solution!

the vision or central idea? Next, move to design development: try out and test some of the ideas as a way to arrive at a finished dish. This is the iterative part. If Francesco is catering a fine-dining dinner party, he will try out dishes and get feedback from his wife, kids, and staff. With his weekly cooking arrangements, the clients will give him feedback to improve or change the dishes. That's a critical part of the process. Francesco claims that,

> You are still subjective as a chef. You may think you have the better solution, but it is really a collaborative approach. Not that everybody's doing the cooking but *you must listen* to that little touch of feedback—it could be a key to the best solution! To me this is the most important part of the design-thinking process. You might get that light bulb in your head, "I should do it that way," and then you make the change.[1]

This is one way to get that moment of inspiration; that intuitive leap in the course of creating something new.

One of the pitfalls of making something, according to both Francesco and conventional wisdom, is that you become emotionally very attached to your work. He says,

> There is a lot of love that goes into making food. You think it's completely right, and then someone tries it and you get a piece of feedback that you just absolutely did not think about, that had not crossed your mind. As a chef, *you can't take criticism personally*, even though you might have a little defensive feeling

for a moment. Take time to *reflect*; you may then have to let that feeling go. It could be that special thing that makes the dish so much better. So, you go back to the drawing board realizing that *your critics may actually have a good point*, and you incorporate their suggestion. I think that's absolutely critical for making good food.[2]

These are great general insights: you must cultivate the maturity and good sense to respond positively to constructive criticism. It is not enough to have a vision and execute it; buy-in from stakeholders is essential. Decisions should be made for the good of a project—or the best solution to a problem—regardless of whose input or ideas are used.

In terms of criticism, Francesco reminds us not to get caught up in the minutia of our designs, rather, revisit the big idea. Everyone's input or feedback should ultimately refer to that vision to be optimally constructive.

When creating a menu, Francesco has a limited amount of time in the client's home—about six hours (Figure 5.2). He uses analytical thinking to figure out how he's going to execute the dishes in that time frame. He has to decide on one relatively complicated main dish and design the rest of the menu around that one so all the dishes can be executed in the relatively short time. First, Francesco figures out a *hierarchy* of tasks to start the cooking day efficiently: what dish goes on the stove first so that he can finish on time? Every menu presents a different design challenge. After the menu is set, Francesco shops the day before or the morning of the assignment so that he arrives with all the ingredients. Design thinking starts: how is he going to execute five entrées and three side dishes? All of them have different cooking times and techniques; some of them are more hands-on, i.e., lasagna, where he has to budget extra time.

Figure 5.2 Using precedents wisely to trigger ideas is a basic tenet of design thinking. In this case, inspiration may come from existing recipes that can be tweaked, built-upon, and improved.

Source: The author.

Clients with strict dietary concerns present challenges. Unfortunately, it is almost impossible to know how things taste to them. With something like salt, some people have trained their pallets to not need it so much. As previously mentioned, many people are used to that salty flavor; it's expected. So Francesco has to think out of the box to come up with something that could take its place. He has to *empathize* and imagine that he does not have that need for salt, and then analyze. He says, "This is analogous to a Renaissance architect trying to operate in the modern style, which would require a completely different way of thinking."

Low cholesterol and high fiber are other examples. The thinking is similar to finding a salt substitute but these are more ingredient-based. Francesco doesn't have many clients who give him a free ride on cholesterol. There are many different kinds of ingredients and fiber that may help to reduce cholesterol and increase fiber. The creative part is in the artful combination of these ingredients and spices so that they yield exceptional taste.

The most important thing in cooking—and there are many important things—is ultimately how the food tastes. (In architecture, the analogy is how the building is experienced.) If it doesn't taste good, you've failed. The challenge, however, is to be both "healthy" and to taste good. This is where creativity is important. Inspiration may come from existing recipes that can be tweaked, built upon, and improved, or used as a starting point to create new dishes that would meet dietary requirements.

Sometimes Francesco starts from scratch:

> For example, when I have a dinner party with minimal con-straints, someone will say that they enjoy seafood and like fava beans and pasta. That's not really a direction or a recipe. My wheels begin to spin and I think about what goes well with fava beans that I've had in my life ... they said fish so I'm thinking that would be great with crab; they said pasta, which would go great in a ravioli. I'll use a lot of flavor memory, then I'll go to books and get images for inspiration. I'll go through recipe books and not think about a specific recipe but maybe there's a flavor that goes with another flavor that I've seen in a book, and that will lead me to add something else to that dish.[3]

> Empathy is a key to transcending a given problem; it facilitates formulating questions that expand, illuminate, or otherwise open up the problem.

Using precedents wisely to trigger ideas is a basic tenet of design thinking.

Encountering, recording, and even analyzing precedents while travelling is also a rich source of inspiration for endeavors in just about any field. In Francesco's case, "Travel has given me another layer of flavor memories, some of which are subconscious, some concrete, but they all become part of the thinking, part of the creative process in the background."

Francesco concludes:

> All of this reinforces the story of design thinking. Everything I do—in some way—uses an aspect of design thinking. Even when I get dressed in the morning—those wheels start spinning. You don't have to be formally trained as an architect, chef, or in design to realize the great benefits of design thinking.[4]

EMPATHY AS A MEANS TO INNOVATE IN A PHARMACEUTICAL COMPANY

> Empathy is the component of design thinking that helped us to develop a fresh mindset and a full appreciation for special needs that led to a new way of thinking.
>
> Meredith Kauffman, PhD

This brief story demonstrates that empathy is one of the most important elements of design thinking. Empathy is a key to transcending a given problem; it facilitates formulating questions that expand, illuminate, or otherwise open up the problem.

Developing meaningful empathy for stakeholders is a remarkable tool for problem definition and, ultimately, solution. A simple commonsense idea that is surprisingly neglected is this: the better we can get to know the people who will be using the spaces, solutions, or, in this case, the products that we design, the better problem solvers we can become, and the more significant the solution.

The design thinker on the team described below essentially assumed the role of stakeholder advocate, serving as a proxy for a typical product user. Armed with primary empathic data, he was then able to propose a wonderful, responsive, and economical solution that *the user could not have imagined*.

Meredith Kauffman, PhD, led research and development projects for a major consumer products company where she focused on using innovative science to design new products to help improve people's health and quality of life. The vignette below describes a snippet from one such project, highlighting the design-thinking process in which defining the right problem to address (in this case, through empathy) is paramount to innovation.

Each brand had a designated open office area called a hub, which accommodated about twenty people. It included specialists in marketing and packaging, research and development (R&D) scientists, and clinical research scientists. It was felt that innovation would be encouraged if people from different disciplines sat together. And indeed there were two designers in the hub. One was a packaging engineer who was expert in the actual make-up of the package and who would follow a project from ideas to production, and hence was frequently away from the team visiting the factories. The other designer was embedded in the team full-time, and was intended to provide inspirational support for the brand.

The project in this case was denture adhesives. The core of the business was adhesives for full denture wearers (people who didn't possess any teeth), but the growth opportunity that was identified by the company was "partials"—for people who required adhesives for small sections that replaced one or two missing teeth. The biggest problem for these consumers was that their appliances didn't fit properly, and, as a consequence, the appliance would wobble and put stress on their teeth. Food particles would lodge under them and cause irritation. That was the initial problem definition from a consumer-need perspective, and also what the team was focused on solving from R&D and marketing standpoints.

After about a month, during one of the team meetings, the designer walked in with a jury-rigged gardening glove, a simulation of what the consumers were going through. He said, "I've been listening to you talk about the consumers, and I've been thinking about their challenges. What you're missing is that you're not hearing them say, 'It's really hard to apply this!'" When they (accidentally) over-applied the adhesives, it was difficult to clean up; the adhesive was essentially a polymer mixed in oil, so consumers would end up with excess oil in their mouths.

The designer pointed out that the team was perhaps failing to address the right problem, which was over-applying the product. It was noted that the adhesives are very viscous products that are squeezed out of a tube. They are much more difficult for this consumer group to squeeze than toothpaste and the designer wanted the team to understand that.

Back to the jury-rigged gardening glove; the designer had attached bits of hard plastic to the fingers on the glove to provide resistance so that it required more effort than usual when squeezing or doing any sort of motion to mimic an arthritic hand. This was intended to give the R&D team an empathic sense of the experience of the typical consumer. While using the glove, it was very hard to properly apply the new products that the team was trying to develop because they were all too thick.

One solution—for partials (using a very viscous experimental product)—was to rethink the original tube design and develop a novel application device. It is similar to a pen clicking; a click would provide a metered dose, which was easier on the arthritic hand, and would not require a squeezing force. With the glove on, it was much easier to click on the prototype device than it was to squeeze from a tube. Another solution—for full dentures—was an easier-to-open and easier-to-squeeze tube (see Figure 5.3).

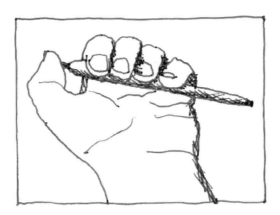

Figure 5.3 Empathy—once again—is so important in helping to discover the salient issues and to focus on the right problem, as exemplified in the development of this device, which provides a metered dose without requiring a squeezing force.

Source: The author.

The caveat that it is absolutely necessary to mention is that there are many different factors that inform product development—not just consumer preference. Cost, for example, is critical to consider on every project. In this case, the redesign of the tube was also an opportunity to address the mandate for cost-cutting.

VISIONING, LISTENING, AND DIAGRAMMING AT A UNIVERSITY

Design thinking can prepare you to accomplish a great deal more than you realize—be open to what those possibilities might be.

James Barker

James Barker, former President of Clemson University, transformed the university by launching major economic development initiatives, raising more than $1 billion in private funding, and leading Clemson through a period of deep funding cuts resulting in a financially healthier institution today than it was before the recession.

Design thinking—particularly *visioning, listening, and diagramming*—had prepared Jim Barker to serve as president of the university in so many ways that it gave him a certain confidence about what he might be able to achieve. The following accounts illustrate how Jim successfully applied these key components of design thinking to his nearly fourteen-year-long tenure as president, and how they can be generalizable to many types of problems.

Visioning

Design thinking enables you to see things that aren't there—as President, Jim claims that visioning was absolutely essential. And then it behooves you to effectively communicate what those visions are, why they are valuable, and why dollars, energy, and time should be invested in those things that do not yet exist. The notion of vision is very important because it provided the campus community with something to critique and rally around, or occasionally advise that the vision—or part of it—was a bad idea.

Jim's vision was that in ten years Clemson ought to be a top-twenty public university in the *US News* ranking. They were seventy four at the time. The board asked Jim and his team to produce metrics. They submitted a report card every quarter, which helped to make it possible to demonstrate that objectives were being met.

During the financial crisis of 2008, Clemson was losing some valuable internships that they prided themselves on having for many of their students. The sponsoring companies were cutting their budgets, so internships were one of the first things to go. How could Jim solve this? In Jim's words:

> I was walking to my office thinking how big an operation the university is. I was looking at a budget that was a billion dollars. I needed a big vision about what's possible with this place and its corresponding budget. We are, in many ways, similar to a small city; we are multifaceted. For example, not only do we teach construction science but we build buildings; not only do we teach about energy and sustainability but we have an energy plant here. Why don't we create internships on campus as opposed to relying on those companies that go up and down? We could create 500 of those internships! We are a complex organization with resources for teaching and offering internships that students can take advantage of. We gave that assignment to our career center and they met the 500 goal.[5]

Jim offers two axioms in support of visioning.

- **The vision requires time to ferment**. "The length of time varies for me. In between sessions, issues keep arising. They stay in my mind, and every now and then there will be a little more insight added to the vision to make it better."

- **An awareness of history and context is critical**.

> I had been thinking of Clemson as my alma mater, which made a big difference because I knew I could effect change if I could make the case that I knew about the University's traditions. If you know about tradition, then you can say, 'I understand all that, now let's make some changes.' If you don't know about tradition, then you're always suspect that you don't really understand the place.

Listening

Jim had to deal with some tremendous challenges due to the 2008 financial crisis in addition to the problem with internships noted above. Jim credits his excellent CFO who urged him to take some dramatic steps to address those challenges. The most difficult intervention was to reduce the salary of everybody on campus by two and a half or three percent, including the coaches. Unfortunately, when that process begins, the state mandates that the directive be applied to everyone, including employees who were below $15,000 in total salary. Even though they were required to follow those guidelines, Jim suggested creating a fund to help their colleagues. He made the first donation and said, "If enough of us contribute, we might be able to help those with the greatest need through this difficult time."

It was almost counterintuitive for Jim to say that he was cutting salaries, and, at the same time, asking that part of each employee's salary (above a certain level) be given to something else that is noble. Jim said,

Design thinking has taught me to know when it is time for patience and when it is time for urgency. I knew this was a time for urgency. So we acted quickly, and recovered relatively quickly as a result of that initiative.[6]

The financial crisis example has to do with listening. Jim admonishes,

We don't listen as well as we should. We want to talk; explain what we have in mind as opposed to the other side of it. I have found that if I could *focus on what someone was saying, and what they were saying between the lines, and what they meant by what they said, not just the words they were using, I could derive great insight*. For example, I could see in the voice and eyes of our CFO that he was not panicked but very concerned. I picked up on that nuance not just by what he was saying, but by what I think he was feeling. That helped me to understand the sense of urgency and how we should begin to address this tremendous challenge. Of course, nobody knew at the time how big it was. The skill that design thinkers have about listening was a tremendous help to me.[7]

Diagramming

Jim draws diagrams very frequently. He prefers to only meet in rooms that have white boards and magic markers. He typically sketches and diagrams as he attempts to work his way through issues, which also serves to illustrate his thoughts to others on the administrative team (Figure 5.4).

Jim asserts that he does his best thinking with a pencil in his hand, making marks on a piece of paper. Sketching or doodling is a precursor to focusing on a problem, then as a means to reaching a solution. Simultaneously thinking and doodling is a great way to start

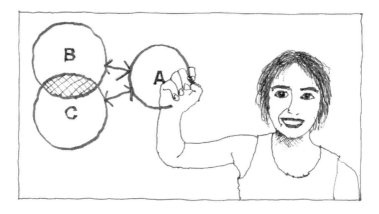

Figure 5.4 Translating information into diagrams that are analytically illuminating can inspire creativity, lead to a deeper understanding of problems, and help to think about possibilities for solutions.

Source: The author.

problem solving. A doodle or mark of any kind—*writing included*—is a symbol of what's going on in one's head.

Jim is giving a talk next month, and, in preparation, he is jotting key words and phrases by hand on paper: a column of ideas that are contrasted with another column of ideas. Then he tries to connect them. The result is a *hybrid between a sentence and a diagram*. And then he includes some diagrams at the bottom of the page. So he ends up with a series of words, phrases, and diagrams that essentially become the preliminary outline for his talk.

Here is an example of how diagramming can be so effective in helping to clarify a problem and solution. Jim was involved in a new initiative called the Clemson University International Center for Automotive Research. It was going to be another campus, in the heart of the region's automobile production, which included

BMW, Michelin, and some others, about forty miles from Clemson. Jim and his team were examining how best to define this project. Jim kept diagramming it as two circles where the academy and business community overlap. The more Jim reflected on the idea, the more he talked to people while showing the diagram. He finally concluded that the two circles do not, in fact, overlap, and that they had to build the connection. They needed to create a bridge between the two circles, and determine what that bridge was going to look like.

That simple diagram freed the team to stop searching for something that didn't exist and redirected their focus. It gave them an energy boost; what should this new creation look like? From there, they were able to build this bridge, the International Center for Automotive Research, which is now thriving. There are six buildings on the campus, with $220 million invested by private corporations in the state. It was very rewarding to see how that thought—as depicted in the diagram—was translated to physical reality.

Jim fervently believes that design thinking can prepare you to accomplish a great deal more than you realize—to be open to what those possibilities might be.

FAST-FAIL AND ITERATIVE

Design thinking—primarily fast-fail and iterative—is provocative in the sense that it doesn't matter if we fail because we're going to get it wrong a bunch of times. But every time we get it wrong, the most important thing is to learn from the experience. That's where the iterative [process of repetition] part comes in. You get it wrong but you learn. And then you get it wrong again but you learn something new. In due course, you will get to a point where you have fewer mistakes, you have learned much, and you are willing to create something from this methodology.

Diego Ruzzarin

Diego Ruzzarin is a world-renowned food design expert and CEO of Foodlosofia, a company that creates profitable, scalable, and sustainable business models for the food and beverage industry.

Problems with problem solving in a corporate context

Diego says, "I'm a big fan of 'fast-fail and iterative'." Why? Because, coming from a corporate background, he learned that certain methodologies become more like an insurance policy and a burden than a guideline, booster, or motivator for project creativity. He believes that people tend to use conventional and ultimately unproductive methodologies and a good chunk of time to justify their pay or to protect themselves from potential disasters.

Business as usual is often related to the democratization of ignorance. There are a lot of people at the table to make decisions; everybody is very polite, inclusive, and nice so what happens is that, most of the time, the *dumbest* people sitting at the table are the ones who make the decisions on a default basis. This is so because everyone has to level-down their thinking in order to be inclusive and so that everyone agrees. In this sense of democratization, *most of the great ideas are lost*. This is closely related to adversity or fear of failure.

An example of fast-fail iterative

The best solutions arise from examining the whole problem, accounting for many variables—not just one piece of the problem. Diego's frustration related to creativity and big companies is that people tend to promote fragmented solutions rather than considering the big picture. In the food industry, ninety percent of the effort to improve products is on flavor. But that is not the whole picture. There are many other variables that are more important than flavor. Nevertheless, research and development spending is so focused on flavor that they almost lose any sense that the other variables exist.

Here is an example. Foodlosofia was hired by a major snack company to work on a specific cheese snack for which the market was shrinking; consumer acceptance was fading. The connection between the brand, product, and traditional consumer was very fragile. When Foodlosofia pushed them to innovate and create new products in this category, they would always play it safe and not want to move beyond the traditional products they sell.

Diego explained that doing concept design—creating new products and formulating new ideas—is not really expensive. If they do this now and fail, it is not important because it is just design—prototypes that can be modified. It will take a couple of months, but eventually they will get something right. The cost of developing the propositions is almost nothing compared with the potential for success. But if they play it safe and stay on this negative trend, it will inevitably be harmful to their market and business.

The snack company trusted Diego's judgment and said, "Okay, let's try it; you have six months to think differently and to innovative in a different direction." Foodlosofia took that liberty, and, even though it was controversial, concluded that they could no longer sell this type of cheese snack to children as originally intended. Instead, the approach was to try to position them and design a new collection of cheese snacks directed to adults—the adults who were originally in love with the brand fifteen years ago, but who are now older. They are in a different moment in their lives; they have different priorities, needs, and life styles. Their expectation from these cheese products is fundamentally different. So the company said, "It's a big bet, but let's try it."

Foodlosofia then created a new collection of products and tested them with consumers. They had excellent results from adults, who said,

> It's great to see these new products because when I go to the supermarket to look for my traditional cheese snacks, I see all this promotion for young people—they are trying to appeal to millennials. I can't relate to the story-telling and to the products anymore, but I used to love the experience. What happened? You lost me in translation.[8]

So Foodlosofia reintroduced the product that is now also relevant to adults, and they immediately fell back in love with the story and brand, and they rediscovered why they used to love these products in the first place.

Diego has psychologists on his team who work with consumer research. The team learned from fast-fail at the beginning of the process. They talked to children to see why they were not connecting to these products anymore. Diego recalls one key response that epitomized learning from failing. The team asked the children why they don't eat these cheese snacks anymore—they used to love them, what happened? Are they not tasty anymore? Is the texture a problem? Is the packaging, graphics, or brand no longer appealing?

The children said no to all of those questions. They said that they take a break while at school in the morning. If they eat these cheese snacks their fingers will be messy and they can't use their cell phones properly, so they'd rather not buy them. Such a simple, rational response yet nobody took the time to *engage and empathize* with consumers, to listen to consumers, to users who say that snacks are important but that, in this instance, they declare that cell phones are much more important today (Figure 5.5).

It was critically important for Foodlosofia in this case to have a fast-fail attitude because they encountered myriad problems, barriers,

Figure 5.5 Why were children not connecting with the cheese snack products anymore? The response epitomized learning from failure.

Source: The author.

consumers, and situations, and from *all* of these variables, they were able to determine how to make the market healthy again.

Dissecting the process

Fast-fail begins with client input, which can vary tremendously, and often cannot be predicted by established marketing algorithms. Here are examples of a wide range of client issues, preferences, and goals. How can new technology provide new products? Our market is fading —do we need to change the market or reposition the category? Do we need to create a new brand to position this product? Our brand is migrating to a new category—we used to do ice cream, now we want to do muffins—is that transition of value? Can you provide a concept and menu for a new restaurant for this type of food and customer-type? Can you help us to create a unique olive oil product?

Normally this client input is accompanied by a great deal of data. Companies provide big data but they rarely know how to use it. So the first part of Foodlosofia's data analytic process is called "understand," which has two components: client-provided information and research that they undertake. Diego has a team of what he calls "philosophers," who are spread around the world, and that form a network of people who are very critical in their mindset about the future of food. When Foodlosofia starts a project, they try to understand the context:

> What are we doing here? We are reinventing the future of ice cream. Let's think about ice cream. What is ice cream today? What does the data tell us? What do we believe are the trends happening around the world that would impact the future of ice cream?[9]

Then the team comes together in an agreement—a mountain of intellectual capital that they all understand. From there, they jump to conclusions. Even if the outcome might be a disaster, they jump to conclusions:

> This is ice cream today. We believe ice cream in the next ten years is going to be about nature. We prototype this category for what ice cream would be like in the next five years: we say this is what ice cream will look like, these are the new technologies that are going to impact ice cream, these are the types of brands that are going to be big, and these are the new business models and distribution systems that are going to change the way the industry works in ice cream.[10]

Then they prototype that reality.

The client is part of *some* of these discussions, not all of them. Most of the time, clients have internal discussions where they believe they know everything; because they have been doing things the same way for thirty years, out of fear, they assume things are not going to change. Foodlosofia keeps them out of some of the conversations, and they take poetic license to explicitly say things the client doesn't necessarily want to hear, and that ostensibly originate with the users of the product in question.

Foodlosofia engages in two types of prototyping: macro and micro. Macro prototyping is what they call scenario design. They provide a holistic simulation of the entire business environment because food design incorporates much more than the food itself. It includes the business model, distribution systems, branding, packaging, the product itself, and understanding the customers—their cultural development and lifestyle. Macro prototyping is, essentially, the context of a new category. Micro prototyping, on the other hand, dives into the specifics of the project, which normally happens on the third or fourth iteration of the process.

In macro prototyping, the first test is presenting to the client (not yet to consumers). For example, Foodlosofia sets forth what they think will happen to the ice cream category in the next five years. They ask if it makes sense: which elements from the future reality do they believe are real, and which of those do they want their business to embrace? Some of the responses are inevitable, i.e., simplicity of ingredients, transparence of origin and process, equality of players in the supply chain.

Then Foodlosofia asks if they believe the speculation that ice cream is going to be a heightened social category that will be more related to alcoholic drinks than to kids. There is also a stake in the ground saying that they want this to be the case; this is where they want to take the category. Some companies may still target children, but they believe there is an unexplored area that will grow: ice creams mixed with alcohol in the happy hour, and a salad with a scoop of rum ice cream. Foodlosofia believes this is the future.

Everyone now has a clear understanding of the idea. The team conducts more research, and talks to consumers, potential clients, and those in the supply chain. They understand enough to launch into micro prototyping: what are the types of products that are needed? Does the technology to make them exist? Do the packaging and brands exist? Can the types of flavors that are promised be developed? Is the texture what it should be? Then eatable prototypes of the new products are developed—something that has color, aroma, flavor, texture, and that can be put in your mouth to see how it melts. Something new is learned from this prototype.

The next layer of testing is with consumers: does this product make sense? Is it the right size, flavor, aroma, brand, storytelling, etc.? Something new is learned from the responses, and adjustments are made for a final round of prototyping: create a new brand, modify the packaging, change the price point. This final round includes three out of fifteen products that are ready to go to the market. Five of the fifteen products will go to the market in year two, two products in year four, and the balance in year five.

Foodlosofia creates this type of innovational roadmap so the company knows when to launch the new products. The vision of the category and the business is established, and changes related to the category are specified to arrive at their target level during the next five to ten years.

Diego has a "triple-headed mentality" that is floating above this iterative process to account for the other variables beyond just flavor. He has three types of professionals working on his team at all times. First, there are two types of designers: graphic (for branding, communication, and packaging) and food (for ingredients, texture, and aroma). The second head on his team is about strategy. Does the idea translate to good business, does the funding make sense, is the pricing system right, do people buy this product—is it affordable? The third head is the psychologist, who strives to be totally objective, and is impervious to foolish ideas and inaccurate statements. Both the design and business model can be great, but the psychologist can be nasty and say that it doesn't make any sense. And everyone needs to hear this reality check.

Diego cites an example. There was a recent presentation at an international conference about a chicken-flavored nail polish that Kentucky Fried Chicken (KFC) just released. It's interesting! It's wow! People are aroused by the idea that fingers can taste just like KFC. It makes sense because fashion items are expensive; it is likely that KFC doesn't have high margin on their products, so having one very high margin product seems like a good idea. A psychologist would ask, "Does it make any sense? You can make it, you can make money, but do you need to make it? Does it help us to progress as humanity?"

Most of the time people seem to lack common sense when they do this sort of thing. They get trapped in fragmented realities when they say something like,

> I need to find eatable packaging, because if I discover this, it will be a panacea—the right medicine for every problem in the food industry. We are criticized because of wasting plastic. If I discover eatable packaging, then I don't have any more disposal issues.[11]

And the company says it makes sense. . ..

DINNER CONVERSATION AS A MODEL FOR EFFECTIVE INTERVIEWS

Recognizing that the interviewee paused for a moment, and the way they paused; or changed affect or emotion—the nonverbal expressions need to be acknowledged and investigated to get to the important insight.

Scott Phillips

Interviews provide a means to deeply understand an issue, problem, or even a proposed solution. Gaining insights, or learning anything valuable from an interview for that matter, requires great skill and a plan. Scott Phillips regards interviews, which are a crucial tool for his business SearchLite, as a special kind of design problem. SearchLite is a market discovery and validation platform—the company helps inventors, entrepreneurs, and growth companies to discover which markets to address first, and which key factors will influence their ultimate market success. Their service includes an "iterative process that integrates key findings from phone interviews, secondary research, and on-line engagement." The process description below, which focuses on the interview, is generalizable to many situations that require insights from interviewing.

Scott's customers are usually technology transfer offices at universities. Anytime a professor invents something that may have commercial value, it must be disclosed to the university's tech transfer department. The faculty inventor(s) then work with this department to explore the commercial potential of the invention, either by licensing it or building a company around it.

Before the university allocates funds for provisional patenting, patenting, or prototyping, which are expensive, they want to know if anyone really cares about the invention, and, if so, why and how much. The professor is married to the idea, has been working on it with a grant for the last twenty years, but they don't know how to get it out of the building or talk to anyone in the real world to see who cares.

Enter Scott's company. For every client or invention, they interview fifteen to twenty people, do secondary research, and report back on its commercial viability: there is either a product/market fit or there isn't. The intention is to render—very quickly—an objective opinion based on the voice of the market. This is accomplished primarily through phone interviews; they are listening for the problems—not selling the solution.

Design thinking is applied in the way that interviews are conducted. Whereas others might conduct a structured interview using an interview guide, SearchLite has a thirty-minute dinner conversation with people. The interviewers are trained in the art of listening specifically for, or digging deep into, tasks that the interviewee is trying to accomplish, professionally or personally, and why. They listen for an outcome, a metric, and a direction. For example, they are listening for: "I wish my dishwasher could clean two times better in one-third of the time." However, the interviewee will not usually quantify that initially, so the skill is to continue asking probing questions such as, "Could you say more about that?" "What did you mean by that?" or "What quality level and how fast?"

Scott's interview method to probe deeply for best understandings is derived from Steve Blank, who was a forefather of the lean startup movement. The idea is to know when to let a conversation wander a little bit, when to focus it, when to probe more deeply, and when to move on.

Another point is to be alert for (and avoid) confirmation bias. For example, if you invented something and you are conducting the interviews, you are undoubtedly listening for everything that you believe to be an endorsement of your solution. It is difficult to *listen objectively* without recognizing your own mental or behavioral biases. In SearchLite's case, the interviewers are trained to not have an opinion going into any solution that they are evaluating.

SearchLite always has two people on every interview; one conducting it and one taking notes. Both hear and interpret what was said, with the moderator focusing on talking to the interviewee. Without the appropriate follow-up questions as a function of listening well, there would be a much more superficial set of takeaways from the same thirty-minute phone call.

The raw ingredient of their deliverable is conducting great phone interviews that have deep insights. They don't necessarily cover a scripted list of twenty questions in a structured format because they will miss the "aha" moment or the insight. Their job is to do fifteen of those interviews with relevant people and look for trends and common key takeaways.

Active listening is a noteworthy skill. Scott references Stephen Covey's *The 7 Habits of Highly Effective People* (Franklin Covey Co., 1998) in which listening with the intent to understand instead of only listening with the intent to respond is underscored. For example, recognizing that the interviewee paused for a moment, and the way they paused; or changed affect or emotion—the nonverbal expressions need to be acknowledged and investigated to get to the important insight.

In sum, the best insights from interviews require the art and skill to find the right person to talk to, knowing how to conduct a thirty-minute conversation, knowing what to listen for, and how to synthesize that across multiple interviews.

But there is more. Part of the process occurs in parallel to the primary phone interviews. SearchLite has researchers who examine what transpired in the interviews—what is not clear or what needs validation. So their challenge is uncovering secondary research and background to add clarity to material that is muddled from the interviews. This allows them to accelerate the process. Subsequent interview questions are modified as a function of what is learned in secondary research. Likewise the secondary research challenges are modified when something new is learned in an interview.

The interviews evolve. The fifteenth interview will be very different from the first in two ways. One is that the person they are talking with in the fifteenth interview is spot-on. The reason they are spot-on as a subject matter expert is because at the end of every interview the interviewers inquire about other people with whom they should be talking. The first three people they talk to are not the right people, but they are close enough that they know someone who is better-suited to talk about the subject. Several more interviews later, they have more referrals from the last set of experts, and eventually they will be talking to the person who is at ground zero for the topic. The other thing that is different is that they are five weeks smarter about asking the right questions. The best interviews, therefore, are always at the last moments of the last few interviews.

The information from the beginning interviews is not at all discounted because it is a process of validation, i.e., how frequently a point is made. The last person really places the information or insights in context.

It's hard to discern patterns if the interviews are all different. However, that underscores the importance of another skill set necessary for good interviews: synthesizing the key findings. A symptom of a bad interview occurs when the interviewer does not review notes for a few days after the interview and didn't have a second person taking notes. It becomes stale and it is easy to forget the most impactful insights. Even though there may be copious notes, it still behooves the good interviewer to write down what they just heard—those insights and impressions—immediately following the interview when it is still fresh.

After every interview, all the notes are culled into one document with the top five takeaways highlighted at the beginning. Once a week, the team brainstorms on the three or four interviews from the past week; then compares all the insights from prior weeks. They are placed in three categories: critical, very important, and important—everything else is background or simply not relevant. So every week they force themselves to have only three insights in each of those categories, which is somewhat arbitrary, but it forces synthesis. At the end of the consultation they want to tell the client that they need to address *three* insights.

Scott equates the reexamination of the interview questions with the iterative process of design thinking. When they check in with the client every week, they summarize what has been learned, and the client can say they know enough about that issue so they can proceed to another one. In that sense it's iterative. Each week the client can direct them to iterate deeper on this topic or pivot to a new one, based on the findings of the previous interviews (Figure 5.6).

Figure 5.6 Developing new interview questions that probe more deeply or pivot to a different issue based on findings from previous interviews is very much analogous to the iterative process of design thinking.

Source: The author.

It is critical to acknowledge an interviewee's time. With permission of the client, SearchLite provides a summary of key findings to each person who speaks with them as a courtesy (in lieu of an honorarium). They generally limit the interview to thirty minutes. And, as a final note, they are sure to end the interview cordially and ask if the interviewee would mind a follow-up; the usual response is that they will either make more time or respond to further questions via email.

NOTES

1 Francesco Crocenzi, [phone] interview by the author, September 1, 2016.

2 Ibid.

3 Ibid.

4 Ibid.

5 James Barker, [phone] interview by the author, March 22, 2016.

6 Ibid.

7 Ibid.

8 Diego Ruzzarin, [phone] interview by the author, October 13, 2016.

9 Ibid.

10 Ibid.

11 Ibid.

6

HEALTH AND
SCIENCE

The problem-solving process can be just as creative and unique as the outcome. The following examples focus on a broad interpretation of design thinking with transcendent results.

Peter Lloyd Jones, PhD, Associate Dean of Design in Medicine at Sidney

Kimmel Medical College, Thomas Jefferson University, believes there is an emerging convergence between the medical and design fields: he claims, "If you train doctors to look at the world through the eyes of a designer, their clinical skills and empathy improve."[1] One of the vignettes below briefly discusses several design projects undertaken by medical students at Jefferson, under the direction of Dr. Bon Ku.

HEALTH CARE DELIVERY

> We, and others, believe that design thinking can be a powerful tool in health care to improve care delivery, train future physicians, and improve the experience for both patients and providers.
>
> Bon Ku, MD, MPP, Anuj Shah, and
> Paul Rosen, MD, MPH, MMM

There is a potentially strong correspondence between medicine, health, and design thinking. Medicine, particularly urban emergency medicine, is about making sense out of multivariate problems in a very compressed time period, and then designing, implementing, and evaluating short- and long-term solutions, again in a compressed time frame. Conceptually, this is a description that suggests design thinking can contribute to creative problem solving in this realm.

The *AMA Journal of Ethics* recently summarized the results of three studies that asserted that those providers who care for the underserved must possess the ability to recognize that the patient may have unexpressed needs, must have an appreciation of local epidemiological factors, knowledge of community resources, and a willingness to take on the role of the patient's advocate. Other necessary skills include the ability to communicate with patients who are from other cultures or speak other languages.[2]

Again, doesn't the above align with some fundamental components of design thinking?

The flavor of the creative component may be very different from that of traditional design, the impact of "art" is clearly not the same, but the challenges are eerily similar.

Another example of the correspondence noted above lies with the Urban Medicine Program of the University of Wisconsin School of Medicine and Public Health. They have developed learning goals that could just as easily be applied to an urban design program in which design thinking is paramount:

- Promoting health equity and reducing health disparities.

- Accessing community resources.

- Enhancing cultural skills.

- Engaging with communities.

- Developing and implementing community-based public health projects, sustaining compassion, promoting wellness, and building resilience.

Dr. Bon Ku et al. further operationalize this general correspondence and congruence. Dr. Ku is an emergency medicine physician and Associate Professor at The Sidney Kimmel Medical College at Thomas Jefferson University in Philadelphia where he teaches design thinking to medical students and serves as director of the design program at the medical college. The program is the first in the US to develop a design curriculum that includes all four years of medical school.

One of the reasons Dr. Ku started the design program for medical students is that he believes physicians lack the toolkit necessary to creatively problem solve within the current landscape of health care delivery. Dr. Ku cites the emergency department where he works as a typical example of many problems in clinical settings today. "It's a very severe, overcrowded space. Patients are stressed, fearful, and anxious; providers are frustrated and stressed as well." Medical students in the design program are working on several projects (among others) to improve both the patient and provider experiences in the emergency department.

With the emergence of design thinking in health-care environments, Dr. Ku no longer views problems as intractable but rather as opportunities to greatly improve health-care delivery. Before this epiphany, states Dr. Ku, many providers, including himself, were skeptical: "We don't have the resources or support, so we're not going to even try to brainstorm or ideate about how to create and implement solutions."

The design process has allowed Dr. Ku's teams to have a safe space to brainstorm, and also the ability to rapidly prototype. Just having an invitation to think of crazy out-of-the-box ideas to develop potential solutions—without considering, at least initially, if they are implementable—is liberating. They relish the chance to sit back with colleagues and students to use a clean whiteboard; to begin to solve the problems they are encountering today.

Recently, a team investigated how they might improve the out-patient services for the family medicine clinic at Jefferson. It's one of the busiest single-site clinics in the country with over 80,000 patients per year. Dr. Ku's team initiated a design workshop with the clinic's providers to fully understand their challenges. One issue is the late patient who shows up 15 minutes after a scheduled appointment, and the resulting stress on the provider, who still has to see that patient—which causes the provider to be late for all the other patients throughout the rest of the day. Business as usual—a slip of paper with the scheduled follow-up appointment and a phone call reminder to the patient—is clearly ineffective.

The team thought about ways to assist patients to arrive on time for their appointments. They interviewed patients and providers, then prototyped and mocked-up potential solutions. They used a story-board technique to propose an app that would message patients at different times before their appointment, reminding them to show up on time. The team did not create anything brand new; there are existing platforms that accomplish the same thing. However, from the interviews with patients, they were able to ascertain that there are optimal times for reminder texts to be effective and to not be perceived as an annoyance. The team was successful in proposing a solution that could be immediately implemented in their family medicine clinic with a simple messaging app for the ninety percent of patients who had smart phones that could receive text messages.

Another recent project with medical students involved creating a journey map of how patients navigate the medical system when they get sick unexpectedly, i.e., when there is stomach pain or high fever for a few days, what does the route to treatment look like? Medical students conducted interviews with Philadelphians focusing on that question.

Profiles or personas of different patient types were extracted from the interviews. Here's an example. A single mother with two children has limited options for health care when she suddenly gets sick. As she is employed full-time, she does not want to take a day off from work, and therefore frequently visited the emergency department during off-hours.

One outcome of the team's work was the creation of an "ecosystem" app chronicling acute unscheduled care that described many different ways patients access health care. It was an exercise in understanding the "end user." Providers describe patients as noncompliant when they don't show up for their appointments. Providers develop treatment plans but don't often understand all the social determinants of their care, and therefore don't really understand the patient and don't specifically tailor their treatment plans. This is an obvious yet illuminating observation for medical students: not all patients are the same. Patient treatment plans should be "designed." Empathizing with the "end user"—a key component of design thinking—leads to better treatment plans for individual patients.

Currently in medical training patients are labeled and blamed as noncompliant when they don't adhere to treatment plans prescribed by providers. A deeper understanding of patients, especially early-on in medical school, will help students to develop more empathy, which will ultimately lead to better care.

Dr. Ku appreciates design thinking because there is a clear methodology that has traditionally worked in product design and service delivery. He believes design thinking can be an effective means for discussing improvements to patient care with colleagues and students. He emphatically states, "Design thinking *amplifies* the standard algorithms that we use."

A DESIGN APPROACH TO TREATING CANCER

> The more scientists learn about cancer, the more diverse and vexing their opponent appears.
>
> Jerome Groopman[3]

Amid star-laden galas and beautiful-people events, we continually declare victories in the "war against cancer." But a hard look at morbidity and mortality data across this daunting landscape of pathology yields a different picture.

Despite the latest science and technology, despite efforts at early detection and aggressive multi-dimensional intervention, despite the authoritative what-to-eat/what-to-drink/how-to-exercise algorithms, despite medicalized websites that purport to bring university labs into *People Magazine* articles, despite all of this, the clinical reality is: human beings with cancer die at essentially the same rates and with the same unavoidable outcomes today as they did decades ago. So, the overarching question is, what do we need to do differently? Recent approaches suggest that *design thinking* with a dose of scientific creativity and courage may provide some desperately needed answers.

Eradicating the spectrum of cancer presents an entire universe of complex problems. Traditional treatments include an array of chemotherapies, surgery, radiation, nanodelivery systems, and genetic and immunologic manipulation. The goal with these treatments is to destroy or remove cancer cells. While there are often impressive results, the treatments do not always result in long-term remission and many have significant side effects.

Elucidating a new treatment pathway for disease is the most basic challenge, the design problem in this case. Inspiration can come from just about anywhere, even from unrelated disciplines, which enables us to examine problems from a fresh perspective. Then we build on the idea, taking it through iterative loops to produce new information, thinking, and questions for a successive loop.

Reframing the question is another tactic in design thinking that facilitates new ways of examining a problem. Instead of, "Is there another, creative way of effectively destroying or removing cancer cells?" we might ask, "*What if* there is a different, perhaps better, means to achieve remission in a given case?" Articulating questions can be extremely valuable, whether or not they lead in a fruitful direction. Posing the right questions is a component in the design-thinking

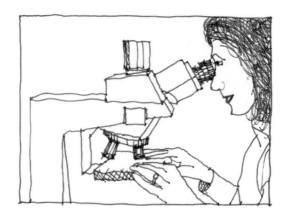

Figure 6.1 Reframing questions can shed light on possible new directions toward finding a solution. For example, instead of: "Is there another, creative way of destroying or removing cancer cells?" we might ask, "What if there is a different, perhaps better means to achieve remission in a given case?"

Source: The author.

loop that can be weighted heavily in the process to provoke a creative response. And be mindful to pose questions that may be counterintuitive—or completely off the wall—to elicit the most potentially innovative responses (Figure 6.1).

Cultivating an optimistic and confident attitude, one that assumes success—that there is in fact the possibility of a new avenue toward a solution—is fundamental to design thinking and advancing the work. Sometimes you have to believe you can do the impossible in order to do the impossible and innovate.

One example of confident and innovative thinking involves an approach to *transform* the cancer cells, not destroy them. Dr. Jerome Groopman describes this exciting new research in his September 15, 2014 article in *The New Yorker*, "The Transformation." Groopman explains that some types of cancer cells, treated with retinoic acid (which is related to Vitamin A), can be transformed to healthy maturity. Practice today combines this method with a second drug that then destroys the now vulnerable mature cells.

The original idea was developed by a researcher in Shanghai, who was inspired by Confucius:

> If you use laws to direct the people, and punishments to control them, they will merely try to evade the punishments, and will have no sense of shame. But if by virtue you guide them, and by the rites you control them, there will be a sense of shame and of right.[4]

Herein lies the creative trigger for the big idea—*from an unexpected source in an unrelated domain*. Groopman quotes the researcher who developed a metaphor: "If cancer cells are considered elements with 'bad' social behavior in our body, 'educating' rather than killing these elements might represent a much better solution." Researchers are continuing to build on this new strategy of treating patients and controlling and normalizing the life cycle of some cancers without actually destroying cancer cells.

Obviously, specific and investigational treatment plans are far more complicated and individualized than suggested here, but the point is to demonstrate how bold new ideas can evolve from a different way of thinking.

NOTES

1 Ben Schulman, "Biology by Design," *Architect*, 2017, 106 (2): pp. 61–62.

2 Brendan M. Reilly, Gordon Schiff and Terrance Conway, "Primary Care for the Medically Underserved: Challenges and Opportunities," *Disease-A-Month*, 1998, 44 (7): pp. 320–346; Wendy Hobson, Roberto Avant-Mier,

Susan Cochella, et al. "Caring for the Underserved: Using Patient and Physician Focus Groups to Inform Curriculum Development," *Ambulatory Pediatrics*, 2005, 5 (2): pp. 90–95; and Robert Blankfield, Michele Goodwin, Carlos Jaen and Kurt Stange, "Addressing the Unique Challenges of Inner-City Practice: A Direct Observation Study of Inner-City, Rural, and Suburban Family Practices," *Journal of Urban Health*, 2002, 79 (2): pp. 173–185.

3 Jerome Groopman, "The Transformation: Is it Possible to Control Cancer Without Killing It?" *The New Yorker*, September 15, 2014 (see www.newyorker.com/magazine/2014/09/15/transformation-3).

4 Ibid.

7

LAW

Thomas Jefferson was unique among US presidents as he was both a lawyer and an architect (and mastered other disciplines as well). Did he apply his design skills to write the Declaration of Independence or as President? Perhaps we'll never know, but in any case there are lawyers today who believe that design thinking greatly facilitates the way they confront situations in their legal practices.

The following two narratives describe how lawyers can apply design thinking in remarkably fresh and unique ways. One way is to use design thinking to help identify the ultimate problem or issue rather than accepting what a client says at face value. Another way design thinking spurs creative thought is by essentially forcing deeper thinking by developing alternative solutions, and then involving the client in discussing their respective pros and cons. And, finally, never losing sight of the need to maintain a certain integrity to the "big idea" when developing a legal structure for any kind of situation is invaluable.

PROBLEM DEFINITION

> Design thinking in a legal context is as much about problem definition as problem solving.
>
> Charles R. Heuer

Chuck is a principal in The Heuer Law Group based in Charlottesville, Virginia, and Cambridge, Massachusetts, and is a mediator/arbitrator for the American Arbitration Association.

According to Chuck, lawyers occasionally employ a methodology that is too rigid. For example, when a client wants to litigate, a typical response is: prepare complaint > determine the parties involved > imagine every legal wrong > proceed with all of them. The cost for that approach is great; the relative return is de minimis. Lawyers don't usually discriminate; clients may spend $50 to protect against a $5 problem.

Another scenario is that after the realization that a good outcome is unlikely, a decision is made to terminate after there is a substantial investment in legal services. Critical thinking and discrimination should occur at the beginning, not after funds are spent; otherwise the outcome could be an elegant solution to the wrong problem.

Chuck believes that many attorneys don't think about other, perhaps more fruitful, approaches. Instead of following the usual or expected protocol (invoking the fairly rigid methodology noted above), Chuck encourages stepping back from the situation and thinking deeply about the context and circumstances. He maintains that, "Design thinking in a legal context is as much about problem definition as problem solving." Therefore, identifying alternate problems that may in fact be more relevant to the situation should be a priority.

When a client presents a problem, an immediate initial response should be, "Is that really the problem? Is there something else that we can solve that will make it go away?" Chuck implores us to *question the problem in order to find the most appropriate solution*. Reflect on what is being said by the client. Try a different angle; evaluate it; then proceed or not. The most powerful solutions ignore the noise, avoid the confusion, and are not corrupted by doubts and misunderstandings.

In other words, do not accept the problem at face value; challenge it. The problem might turn out to be the actual problem as initially presented, but, in any case, the problem as stated should not be considered a given. Focus on trying to ascertain a global under-standing of the situation to find the right problem. For example, in architecture, the answer may not necessarily be a new building, instead it might be renovating existing space to be more efficient, or scheduling the use of spaces differently, and so on.

Ask probing questions to find the real problem. Be naturally skeptical; take in everything with a grain of salt. Keep your mind open to look for something seemingly unrelated to the problem for inspiration. Look for connections. For example, Chuck cites a litigation case in which a woman fell going down steps, and mentioned [during a deposition] to the lawyer for the defendant that her daughter was getting married. Picking up on this seemingly unrelated fact, a video was discovered of the woman who fell on the steps dancing at the wedding *after* the incident, providing sufficient evidence that she was not injured as she had claimed.

Chuck has a fascinating take on the iteration component of design thinking: *dialogue as iteration*. The dialogue is part of the iterative loop: conversing back and forth several times as a means to get to the core issues. You can become wiser and improve the case with greater understanding with each successive loop.

Establishing a productive dialogue with an adversary is crucial. Figure out the underlying interest in a certain position. One way to do that is to explain your concerns related to a position with the expectation that the other party will then open up. Model the behavior to jump-start the dialogue (or, follow the cliché and give some to get some).

ALTERNATIVES AND THE BIG IDEA

The power of visual thinking is immense.

The notion of alternatives is an extremely valuable part of design thinking.

Stepping back and always asking yourself what's the big idea— what is the organizing principle to what you're doing—is a key part of design thinking.

Jay Wickersham

Jay Wickersham is principal of the Cambridge, Massachusetts, law firm Noble, Wickersham & Heart LLP. Jay holds both law and architecture degrees from Harvard.

There are three ways that design training has been helpful to Jay. One is the synthesizing of different kinds of information from a whole host of different sources. Design thinking is very powerful in training you to *keep looking more broadly; to keep looking beyond the borders of what one might think is the problem*. Draw in information and knowledge from all kinds of different sources. In that sense, design training is quite the opposite of legal training. In legal training you are trained to screen things out, to keep narrowing down, and to make a decision that turns on one or two key legal points, so you can dismiss everything else as irrelevant.

In contrast, design thinking stipulates that you look as broadly as possible, and then find ways to integrate the information you've gathered. Related to that point, in architecture you come to *respect the perspective and expertise of others*. Architects have a unique responsibility to coordinate vast amounts of multidisciplinary input: on any project of modest scale architects might have from ten to thirty or more consultants in other disciplines, any one of whom knows more about their part of the project than the architect does.

And the same thing is true when it comes to the contractor. Any one of those subcontractors and suppliers know more about their particular piece of the building than the architect. So the architect's challenge is to extract that expertise, weigh it, and figure out how to coordinate that particular piece of information with all the other pieces of information.

Here is an example of how Jay operationalizes that from his law practice. They do a lot of work in ownership transitions, helping architects reorganize their firms, and help the next generation to come forward and take on responsibility, and, ultimately, ownership. The legal part of that absolutely has to go along with the financial side. So, whenever they work on succession planning, there is always a very close partnership with the accountants. Jay is very aware that accountants have the expertise in the finances of the firm as well as tax implications. Jay's job is to understand; to be able to ask the right questions. Very often Jay realizes that he becomes the translator—he explains to his clients what the accountants are saying. He puts it in simple English. His role is to gather, synthesize, and then translate that information, and he does this on a regular basis.

Another valuable skill from design thinking is the ability to think and communicate graphically and visually. This is not at all about incredibly elaborate three-dimensional modeling or rendering, but, rather, very simple kinds of diagrams. One of the things Jay believes is invaluable is, whenever possible, to translate legal information to some graphic form, i.e., charts or diagrams. This is a way to harness and present complex information to a nontechnical audience in a simple straight-forward way. *The power of visual thinking is immense, and has the potential to help everybody.* Jay is a huge fan of Edward Tufte, who has authored numerous books (such as *Envisioning Information, Beautiful Evidence*, and *Visual Explanations*) on graphically presenting information. (I would add that diagramming is not only helpful to the audience or reader, but also to the design thinker as a tool to conceive of potential solutions. See Part 1 for elaboration on this point.)

A second extremely valuable part of design thinking that Jay has learned is the notion of alternatives. Do not fall in love with your idea. You need to generate five more. Jay is always trying to give his clients alternatives, whether it's figuring out how to resolve a dis-pute, structuring contracts on a complicated international project, or thinking about an ownership transition. List the pros and cons of each of the alternatives or approaches. Jay, of course, has a sense of which he thinks is favorable, but this should also be a discussion with the client.

If there are several options, the final solution, scheme, or alternative usually borrows elements from each one. Jay states that, in his law firm, they don't pretend to have the "right" answer. Whenever possible, they *present alternative approaches as a way of eliciting the discussion* (Figure 7.1), which usually results in coming up with an answer that will be probably better than any of the alternatives. And it will get people on board to support it.

Figure 7.1 Whenever possible, present alternatives (together with their respective pros and cons) as a means to elicit discussion and to arrive at an even better solution.

Source: The author.

Jay believes that if you give people the sense of different options, they don't feel like they're being railroaded into doing just one thing. They are much more receptive to having an open conversation about the pros and cons. If you feel strongly about one option, it is often easier to convince somebody if you've been able to show why one approach is not as strong as another.

Here is the third way that design thinking is so important to Jay: *the way in which the process is iterative*. This is central to design thinking. The process starts at the conceptual level—and this applies to the alternatives as well—but keeps narrowing in. When Jay is putting together contracts or some legal agreement, he'll make the analogy that they don't want to jump into construction documents before they've done the concept design—and the client is asking him to move right into construction documents. The concept design must be completed first, then fleshed-out in the next phase, and then they can move into the actual agreement.

There's a real risk, particularly when someone has an expertise (i.e., a lawyer), that a client assumes you're going to move directly into the final product. In design thinking you start conceptually and then flesh it out, develop more detail, and then, as you move into a larger scale, you are forced to tackle a whole new set of issues. Note that always, through all iterations and scales, you must try to maintain a kind of integrity to the design or big idea. That's a wonderful model for a process and end result. Jay keeps that in mind when developing a legal structure for any kind of situation.

In terms of resolving disputes, a classic mediation technique is to find the places where there is agreement; start in the areas of agreement and, if there are disagreements, table them. Once the agreed-to areas are established, that constitutes a basis for people to work together. This is a great strategy for formulating the "design" of a solution or a project.

> Always asking yourself what is the big idea, what is the organizing principle to what you're doing—is a key part of design thinking.

With a design, there are times when you know there are certain parts that are just not working. Leave that part of it alone for a while, and develop the parts that are working, then come back to the problem areas. For example, Jay's wife, who is a writer, was working on a book and had a lot of fantastic material but she knew that the overall structure wasn't really developed. She needed some organizing thread. She finally came up with an idea that she thought might be effective, but wasn't sure. Jay opined that she should use it, almost arbitrarily, as an organizing device or parti. At the very least it would help her to gain control over the material, and wrestle with how the project could be organized. If it works—great. If not, abandon it, but know that it has been a useful exercise.

Jay thinks that the idea of stepping back and always asking yourself what is the big idea, what is the organizing principle to what you're doing—is a key part of design thinking.

8

WRITING

acing the blank piece of paper and being blocked is something many writers—novices and veterans alike—have experienced. Design thinking can facilitate inspiration, and help to unlock ideas and express them artfully in writing.

One of the best and most helpful analogies of writing to design thinking is to consider the draft (and subsequent versions) as prototype for testing and evaluation. Then the iterative loop is repeated, as critical feedback may trigger anything from a completely different tack to only minor modifications.

DRAFT AS PROTOTYPE

> Every time you test a draft (or prototype) you may actually change the question you're working on—and that's what makes it design thinking—as opposed to straight hypothesis testing or research.

> Mark Childs

Mark Childs is Associate Dean and Professor in the School of Architecture and Planning at the University of New Mexico, and the author of a half-dozen award-winning books.

Mark considers the iterative process of design thinking—or the repeating loop of tasks leading to prototyping—as fundamental to writing. In design-thinking language, the draft is the prototype that gets evaluated. You write something and then test it in different ways at different phases—or drafts. For example, sending a preliminary draft to trusted advisors and also to *un*trusted advisors to provide feedback. Another way to test the prototype/draft is to review it carefully to ensure that it makes logical or emotional sense. Imagine an inverted cone with a spiral going up on the outside—the top is where the prototype is made, which goes down for testing; then repeating: making and testing, and so on. Every time you test a draft (or prototype) you may actually change the question you're working on—and that's what makes it design thinking—as opposed to straight hypothesis testing or research.

> The aspect of design thinking that best applies to writing is crystallizing the central issue; determining what is really at stake.

Mark believes that the aspect of design thinking that best applies to writing is crystallizing the central issue; determining what is really at stake. It's part of the process of starting down a path without necessarily knowing where it goes. There are branches along the way, and it is not clear which ones to select. So you go down some, and then you backtrack; then you go down some others.

Putting ideas and thoughts down in writing helps you to get to another place. You may start out with one kind of general approach but the writing itself tells you that you're going somewhere else. It's almost like a point of departure for further exploration. Novelists talk about this effect in which the characters start writing the story. It's analogous to designing a building where you are truly listening to what the client wants, what the site "wants," what the constraints dictate from the budget, contractors, and city—all this is context. And once you start *playing* in that context, you have a much better idea of the real question or what the essence of the work should be. Mark reiterates that you don't necessarily know where this exploration will lead before you start. This is an example of one of the basic tenets and a recurring refrain of design thinking—comfort with ambiguity.

Closure on an iterative process is ultimately a personal judgment. It's not as though you arrive at the right answer. Design thinking is not like a math problem or a scientific experiment when you know it's complete. You could always add some other criteria or refine or change the question a little bit, or try to do a little more. So how do you know whether you are finished? There really isn't an answer—it is a matter of judgment. And this is where aesthetics have some leverage: has the piece gelled? Is it something more than the sum of its parts? Does it have a kind of resonance?

> Aesthetics have some leverage: has the piece gelled? Is it something more than the sum of its parts? Does it have a kind of resonance?

You should always be looking for an aha moment or an intuitive leap. There's something that is gnawing at you, bugging you—completing a draft might just illuminate the issue. When you analyze it, you can immediately see that something is entirely backwards, i.e., let's put the conclusion at the beginning and try it that way. That's what you are looking for: *feedback from the work itself*.

Mark offers a piece of advice for beginning or inexperienced writers. Split your mind in two: for a while just write while putting the editor part of your mind away. Many people are hesitant to put anything down because it's not perfect; but it has to go through the process a few times. Mark says,

> I have a few tricks to help silence my editor. If something comes up, I write a note in the margin and I know I'll get to it later. If I don't have the perfect word, I'll put it in brackets. If I know some thought must go there but I don't quite know what it is, I'll put stars there. The point is to just keep going.[1]

Once you have a draft, switch over to the editor mindset. And look at all those questions and tear it apart. Does it make logical sense? Does it make emotional sense? Can people follow the arguments? Is that the right word? Mark continues to reveal some of his personal process:

> A leap can occur after I've written all this, now that I know what the essential question is and what I should be writing about. A lot of the material then may just go to the side. I might completely re-outline. More leaps—aha moments—can occur

with more experience because you have prepared, and have confidence in the process that there will be a positive outcome, and you trust that the act of writing will get you there.[2]

Underscoring Mark's design-thinking approach to writing, he emphasizes that it is a circular iterative process, not a linear one. It can be characterized by revisiting and putting things out there for more evaluating. Mark often wants to do multiple drafts to compare, contrast, and find out what the issues really are.

After Mark feels somewhat comfortable with the draft, then he has a couple of people he trusts to review it—not just laugh at him when it's in a laughable form—they can look at it and be direct. He will redraft it and develop it further, and then unsympathetic readers can review it. If you don't have a sympathetic reader initially, Mark asserts, it could seriously undermine your confidence about the work.

Mark underscores the need to fully grasp both the content and context of any critique of the work, which includes who is doing the critiquing and their possible agendas. The specifics of the criticism may not be helpful or relevant but it may point to broad issues to address. Pay attention to what the critics are saying that may be problematic about the work, and try to determine the systemic issue. The problem may not be what they pointed to because they don't know as much as you do about the content (i.e., the earlier drafts with their deleted content, and future intentions). They are just pointing to a problem with the current version. So you need to take time to analyze and understand the specific nature of the criticism, and who the critic is: is the critic representative of the target audience? Are they expert in a particular aspect of the topic?

There are many other ways to test the draft. Be sure to remember to keep the audience in mind from the beginning; what's the frame, what's the general purpose? And, near the end, what is the polish so people can read and understand what you wrote? Mark suggests evaluating it from the perspective of a seven-year-old: where would they get stuck, and is that OK? It shouldn't necessarily be changed but should prompt the question, "Am I being too pompous here?" or is there another problem?

Now, judgment comes into play: which one of those evaluations are you going to weigh, and how? That's where your inner voice ultimately rules. Know and interpret the context—the ground in which the work grows—to inform the direction of future drafts or iterations.

Take all criticism with a grain of salt: again, consider the source, and the evidence associated with the critique. One difficult moment is when someone with a very different agenda challenges your work. You must understand that they may have different goals, and then decide whether or not those are valid for the next iteration. Also, be cognizant that a draft is just a draft—it doesn't usually include everything else that's in your head, which is fine because ultimately the thing has to live without you. The closer it comes to completion, the more it is just itself, and you can't be present to defend it on the basis of what you intended to do or what you thought about.

The ideation, brainstorming, or whimsy phase is also part of the writing process. Coming up with a whole bunch of ideas is very useful at the beginning when your internal editor (or client or others) says, "no, you can't." Whimsy is useful to jump-start another approach, and maybe take some approaches off the table.

One of the great attributes of design thinking is that multiple different tools can be used at multiple different iterations. For example, play the roles of people whose style you respect for their perspective on your work. You can pretend in your head that x is critiquing your work: what would they say about it? Model that person in your head. It won't be perfect because what you think they would say and what they would actually say are two different things but, nevertheless, it's an exercise in developing a fresh voice, a set of goals, an approach, or an alternative way of evaluating. The tools you apply from design thinking are a function of the problem, your audience, the context, and who's paying for it.

Mark poses a question—and a reality check:

> How much are you doing the work for yourself versus how much are you doing work on behalf of others? There's always some degree of both, hopefully. If it's mostly about me, and my audience is me, then be aware that this is the potentially myopic stance that some artists take.[3]

If you're having fun writing, that's probably a good indicator that you are taking a reasonable path. If it's complete torture, not in any given moment but for the long-run, then you might want to look at where you're going with it. Terrific advice from Mark, who adds that,

> There are inevitably moments of great torture (i.e., what is that word? How do I reframe this sentence?); it can be incredibly hard at times but that's only a moment. I wouldn't worry so much about a moment, but rather, over a period of time. Does the work have a sense of joy?[4]

WRITING PROSE FOR WRITING PROS

Design thinking as rolling the snowball downhill

> Writing is a labor of love and a struggle at times. But you don't have to solve all the research and writing challenges you encounter all at once. Hold some of the "constraints" at bay while you work on others.

Michael Tardif

Michael Tardif, who was interviewed earlier in Chapter 5, provides a few incredibly insightful tips for writing a book. These tips embody the spirit of design thinking.

Michael told me that he received some really great advice from an experienced author before writing his first book: "Don't start with Chapter 1, Page 1. It will feel, from beginning to end, like rolling a snowball up a hill." Instead, start with the easy material first, somewhere in the middle; that with which you are most comfortable or conversant. It may translate to an entire chapter or just a section of a chapter. Knock it off and put it behind you. Then move on to the next easiest part, incrementally tackling the more difficult subject matter.

If you get stuck on something, whether it's finding the right words or finding the time to research a topic, set it aside (for "reflection" or "creative pause"), and move on to something else. This approach does two things: (1) it quickly builds a sense of accomplishment; and (2) it increases your knowledge and sharpens your thought process, which equips you better for the remaining, more challenging, material, which suddenly won't look so challenging. The newly designed metaphor, then, is to roll the snowball down the hill rather than up the hill.

Instead of dreading the thought of working on the book, you'll look forward to it. It will be fun! As you move forward, you will inevitably go back and rewrite some of your earliest material, but rewriting is always much easier than writing from scratch. This writing/design-thinking process is messy, not linear (and drove Michael's editor nuts), but as long as you know what the "jigsaw puzzle" (your outline) is supposed to look like, it doesn't matter; you'll eventually complete it. You will inevitably revise your outline as you go along too, but, again, you'll be doing that in the context of the overall vision. (See Michael's *strategic-plan-as-jigsaw-puzzle* metaphor in relation to design thinking described in another context in Chapter 5.)

Getting to the aha moment

> You have to try all these iterations in order to discover a great idea.
>
> Charles Linn

Before serving as Director of External Affairs, School of Architecture, Design & Planning at the University of Kansas, Charles Linn was Deputy Editor of *Architectural Record* for over seventeen years.

As Charles undertakes a writing task, possibilities and new ideas emerge from just getting things down on paper, which amounts to a layering of information. It is analogous to design thinking in architecture in that multiple sketches—just drawing things on paper—greatly facilitate the search for an idea. Charles says, "You don't necessarily know what the idea is; you know there is an idea somewhere but you have to try all these iterations in order to discover it!" Charles continues:

> Of course there is the preparation and research, then all of a sudden, the punch line will suggest itself. Or, as I'm writing, I discover new ideas that are in these piles of paper that I don't really know are there when I initially start out. All I know is that I'm passionate about something, or angry about something, and the stuff just bubbles up somehow. A lot of it is just being prepared.[5]

"The solution favors the prepared mind." This quote, paraphrased from Louis Pasteur, is one of Charles' favorites. His sage advice is to absorb all there is to know about the problem, issue, or project and its context. Identify and then fully understand precedents for solving similar or related problems. Drawing upon this reservoir of knowledge will inform and contribute to finding the right solution.

> Find an appropriate metaphor to make people's imaginations take a leap with you.

The iterative process in writing is so important. Charles says that his early drafts are like the brush strokes of what he's doing. He feels that they are usually not very good—perhaps good enough—but to make it excellent he has to keep tweaking and changing it. It's a cliché but one thing leads to another. That's why he tends to write things over and over again.

One reason Charles occasionally has trouble—as do many of us—is that when he really falls in love with something he wrote, he can't redo it or give it up. Infatuation should not get in the way of larger goals, and openness to alternatives (perhaps almost as infatuating but very different) is a hallmark of design thinking, as noted in Part 1.

Charles offers a great brainstorming tip that helps him to write well: find an appropriate metaphor to make people's imaginations take a leap with you. In July 2010, in the midst of the economic downturn, Charles opened a story in *Architectural Record* about the top 250 architecture firms. The metaphor he used provides a different way of illustrating something that hopefully will make people laugh or that will make them feel better about a difficult situation for the profession, where some people lost their jobs. Here is the opening.

> Waiting to find out how much revenue would decline as projects were cancelled and backlogged work ran out has been a bit like watching a fat man start a swan dive off the high board: you want to avert your eyes so as not to see what happens when his flabby midsection smacks the water, but you look on and hope for a graceful landing.[6]

NOTES

1 Mark Childs, [phone] interview by the author, April 7, 2016.

2 Ibid.

3 Ibid.

4 Ibid.

5 Charles Linn, [phone] interview by the author, March 15, 2016.

6 Charles Linn, "Top 250 Architecture Firms 2010: Income Belly Flops; Firms Swim for Work Offshore," *Architectural Record*, July 16, 2010.

INDEX

Page numbers in *italics* refer to figures.